Know It, Show It

GRADE 2

Printed in the U.S.A.

ISBN   978-0-358-19207-7

18 2591 23

4500881900   DEFG

r4.21

Grade
2

Contents

MODULE 1

Week 1 4
Week 2 15
Week 3 25

MODULE 2

Week 1 33
Week 2 44
Week 3 54

MODULE 3

Week 1 62
Week 2 73
Week 3 83

MODULE 4

Week 1 91
Week 2 102
Week 3 112

MODULE 5

Week 1 120
Week 2 131
Week 3 141

MODULE 6

Week 1 149
Week 2 160
Week 3 170

MODULE **7**

Week 1. 178

Week 2. 189

Week 3. 199

MODULE **8**

Week 1. 207

Week 2. 218

Week 3. 228

MODULE **9**

Week 1. 236

Week 2. 247

Week 3. 257

MODULE **10**

Week 1. 265

Week 2. 276

Week 3. 286

MODULE **11**

Week 1. 294

Week 2. 299

Week 3. 304

MODULE **12**

Week 1. 309

Week 2. 314

Week 3. 319

Name _____

Words to Know

Learn these words. You will see them in your reading and use them in your writing.

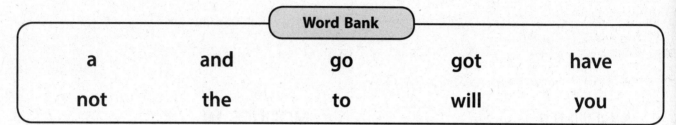

Word Bank

a	and	go	got	have
not	the	to	will	you

▶ Write a word from the box to complete each sentence.

1. Tim has _____ pal.

2. I _____ a pal, too.

3. The pal is _____ a cat.

4. The pal can nip _____ nap.

5. It _____ get big.

6. Do _____ have a pal?

▶ Write sentences that use two other words from the box.

_____

_____

_____

Name _____

Short *a*, *i*

You can spell the short *a* sound with *a*, as in *jam*.
You can spell the short *i* sound with *i*, as in *bit*.

▶ Write each basic and review Spelling Word in the
correct column.

Words with short *a*	Words with short *i*
_____	_____
_____	_____
_____	_____
_____	_____
_____	_____
_____	_____

Spelling Words
Basic
sad
bit
jam
glad
list
win
flat
if
fix
rip
kit
mask
Review
as
his
clap
chip

Name _____

Consonants; Short a, i

The word *cat* has a consonant-vowel-consonant, or CVC pattern.
A word with a CVC pattern usually has a short vowel sound. *Cat*
has the short *a* vowel sound. *Pin* has a short *i* vowel sound.

▶ Write the word that names the picture.

1.

   kid   kit   Kim   _____

2.

   cat   sat   rat   _____

3.

   as   is   in   _____

4.

   pin   nip   pan   _____

5.

   bid   dad   dab   _____

Name _____

Short *a, i*

You can spell the short *a* sound with *a*, as in *jam*.
You can spell the short *i* sound with *i*, as in *bit*.

▶ Write the missing letter in each Spelling Word.
Then write the Spelling Word on the line.

1. s___d	**2.** b___t
_____	_____
3. l___st	**4.** m___sk
_____	_____
5. j___m	**6.** k___t
_____	_____
7. r___p	**8.** fl___t
_____	_____
9. gl___d	**10.** f___x
_____	_____

Spelling Words

Basic

sad
bit
jam
glad
list
win
flat
if
fix
rip
kit
mask

Review

as
his
clap
chip

▶ Which two basic Spelling Words did you *not* write?
Circle them in the list. Then write a sentence that uses
both words.

Name _____

Phonics Review

The word *nap* has a CVC pattern and the short *a* vowel sound.
The word *kin* has a CVC pattern and the short *i* vowel sound.
The word *napkin* has two syllables, or parts. You can blend the
parts to read the word.

▶ Complete each sentence. Use each word from the box once.

> **Word Bank**
>
> cat   did   nab   picnic   rabbit   sat

1. Dan and Pam go to a _____ .

2. Bandit the _____ is at the picnic.

3. Dan and Pam _____ a bit.

4. Bandit _____ not sit.

5. Bandit ran to a _____ .

6. Bandit did not _____ it.

Name _____

Power Words: Match

Word Bank

bellowed	bounce	cool	grinned
handle	might	munch	rough

▶ Write the Power Word from *Clark the Shark* that best fits each item.

1. Which word means almost the same as *smiled*? _____

2. Which word names a way to chew food? _____

3. Which word is the opposite of *gentle*? _____

4. This word means *roared* or *yelled*. _____

5. Which word describes how you act in a difficult moment? _____

6. Which word can mean almost the same as *calm*? _____

7. Which word means that you put all your effort into a task? _____

8. Which word names an up-and-down movement? _____

Words That Describe Actions

Verbs are words that **describe actions.** They tell exactly what someone or something is doing.

▶ For each sentence, circle the word that describes an action. Then write an action word from the box that means almost the same as the word you circled. Use a dictionary if you need help.

Word Bank

dances	drop	gobble	turn	wail	wave

1. Those toys spin fast. _____

2. We eat our snacks. _____

3. The babies cry for their toys. _____

4. Leaves fall to the ground. _____

5. The flags flap in the breeze. _____

6. Maria sways to the music. _____

Name _____

Setting

The **setting** tells where the story happens. It also tells when the story takes place. Understanding why the setting is important will help you understand the story better.

▶ Answer the questions about *Clark the Shark*.

🔍 Pages 18–20 Where do events in the story take place? Why are the changes to the setting important?

_____

_____

_____

🔍 Pages 21–23 Where and when does this part of the story take place? Why do you think the author chose this setting?

_____

_____

_____

_____

_____

_____

Name _____

Antonyms

Antonyms are words with opposite meanings. The words *asleep* and *awake* are antonyms.

> **Word Bank**
>
> dark   dirty   found   late   narrow   sour

▶ Read each sentence. Choose the word from the box that means the opposite of the underlined word. Write it on the line.

1. A <u>wide</u> truck drove into a _____ tunnel.

2. I <u>hid</u> the doll and Molly _____ it.

3. He would rather be too <u>early</u> than too _____ .

4. The apple smells <u>sweet</u> but tastes _____ .

5. In the day it is <u>light</u> but at night it is _____ .

6. Before I washed my <u>clean</u> shirt, it was _____ .

Name _____

Collaborative Conversations

Follow these rules when you have conversations with classmates or teachers. Circle the rules that are easy for you. <u>Underline</u> the rules that you need to work on.

1. Take turns. When someone makes a point, try to add something to his or her ideas.

2. Speak clearly and be polite.

3. Listen carefully and stay on topic.

4. Ask questions when you don't understand something.

5. Decide if you should use formal or informal language.

Name _____

Have a conversation with a friend about a book you read. Talk about this question:

Do you think others should read this book? Why or why not?

After your conversation, answer the following questions.

Did you take turns?	Yes	No	Sometimes
Did you build on what your partner said?	Yes	No	Sometimes
Did you use complete sentences?	Yes	No	Sometimes
Did you speak loudly and clearly?	Yes	No	Sometimes
Were you polite?	Yes	No	Sometimes
Did you stay on topic?	Yes	No	Sometimes
Did you ask questions?	Yes	No	Sometimes
Did you answer with more than one word?	Yes	No	Sometimes
Did you listen with care?	Yes	No	Sometimes

What rule do you need to practice more?

_____

_____

Name _____

Words to Know

Word Bank

best	does	end	job	left
men	more	see	than	wash

▶ Write a word from the box to complete each sentence.

1. The _____ have a pan.

2. They _____ the cab.

3. It is a big _____ .

4. I _____ the men and the rags.

5. A man _____ his best to wash it.

6. This is the _____ cab !

▶ Write two more sentences. Use at least two words from the box that you did not use yet.

_____

_____

Name _____

Short o, u, e

You can spell the short *o* sound with *o*, as in *frog*.
You can spell the short *u* sound with *u*, as in *hug*.
You can spell the short *e* sound with *e*, as in *net*.

▶ Write each basic Spelling Word in the correct column.

Words with short *o*	Words with short *u*	Words with short *e*
_____	_____	_____
_____	_____	_____
_____	_____	_____
_____	_____	_____
_____		

Spelling Words

Basic

yes

job

hug

rest

frog

hum

left

melt

plum

shut

net

dot

Review

glad

fix

jam

list

Name _____

Consonants; Short o, u, e

The word *log* has a consonant-vowel-consonant, or CVC pattern.
A vowel in a CVC pattern usually has a short sound. *Log* has a
short *o* vowel sound. *Hum* has a short *u* vowel sound. *Yes* has a
short *e* vowel sound.

▶ Write two words to complete each sentence.

1. The _____ has not left _____ .

   yet   lot   fix   bus

2. Mel _____ his cab _____ .

   job   gum   quit   pencil

3. Does the bag have a _____ _____
   on it?

   hug   zigzag   red   got

4. Val set a big _____ in the _____ .

   wet   yum   van   box

5. Six _____ ran at _____ .

   men   sunset   nod   happen

Name _____

Short o, u, e

You can spell the short *o* sound with *o*, as in *frog*.
You can spell the short *u* sound with *u*, as in *hug*.
You can spell the short *e* sound with *e*, as in *net*.

▶ Use the code to find the letters in each Spelling
Word. Then write the Spelling Word on the line.

1	2	3	4	5	6	7	8	9	10	11	12	13
a	b	c	d	e	f	g	h	i	j	k	l	m

14	15	16	17	18	19	20	21	22	23	24	25	26
n	o	p	q	r	s	t	u	v	w	x	y	z

1. ___ ___ ___   _____
   4 15 20

2. ___ ___ ___   _____
   25 5 19

3. ___ ___ ___ ___   _____
   18 5 19 20

4. ___ ___ ___ ___   _____
   13 5 12 20

5. ___ ___ ___ ___   _____
   16 12 21 13

6. ___ ___ ___ ___   _____
   19 8 21 20

7. ___ ___ ___ ___   _____
   6 18 15 7

8. ___ ___ ___ ___   _____
   12 5 6 20

Spelling Words

Basic
yes
job
hug
rest
frog
hum
left
melt
plum
shut
net
dot

Review
glad
fix
jam
list

Name _____

Power Words: Yes or No?

Word Bank

panicked   ridiculous   prohibited   cautiously

▶ Read each sentence. Circle **YES** if the word makes sense or **NO** if it does not. Rewrite the sentence so it makes sense.

1. I **panicked** about the great news.

         YES   NO

_____

2. We laughed at the **ridiculous** joke.

         YES   NO

_____

3. Things that are **prohibited** are against the rules.

         YES   NO

_____

4. It's a bad idea to walk **cautiously** on an icy sidewalk.

         YES   NO

_____

_____

Name _____

Author's Purpose

The **author's purpose** can be to **persuade**, **inform**, or **entertain**.
To find the author's purpose, look for clues about the **genre**.
You can also ask questions about what you read and find answers.

▶ Answer the questions about *The Great Puppy Invasion*.

🔍 Pages 35–37 What evidence helps you figure out what kind of
text this is? Why do you think the author wrote the story?

_____

_____

_____

_____

🔍 Pages 42–46 What is the author's purpose for writing this
story? What do you think the author wants readers to learn?

_____

_____

_____

_____

Name _____

Phonics Review

Words with the CVC pattern usually have a short vowel sound. The word *puppet* has two CVC syllables, or parts. Blend the parts to read the word.

▶ Read the words. Three words name things that are alike. Write the word that that does not belong.

1. yak   piglet   ox   cactus   _____

2. ten   wagon   seven   six   _____

3. muffin   pretzel   bag   bun   _____

4. wet   hat   mitten   jacket   _____

5. basket   tunnel   bucket   box   _____

6. puppet   jet   van   bus   _____

Name _____

Words That Describe People, Places, Things

Adjectives are words that **describe** people, places, or things. Some adjectives describe how things look, sound, smell, feel, or taste. Adjectives can also describe what something is like or how it acts.

Word Bank

hard	loud	silly	spicy	tall

▶ Complete each sentence with the best adjective from the box. You can look up words you do not know in a dictionary.

1. The mountain is _____ .

2. I like to watch _____ clowns.

3. The music is too _____ .

4. The soup is very _____ .

5. A snail lives inside of a _____ shell.

▶ Choose one of the sentences above. Write other adjectives that can be used to complete the sentence. Use a dictionary to help you.

6. _____

Power Words: Draw and Write

┌─────────────────────────┐
│   **Word Bank**   │
└─────────────────────────┘

| compliment | elected | local | mock |

▶ Draw a picture or write words that will help you remember each Power Word from *Being a Good Citizen*. Try to write more than you draw.

1. compliment

2. elected

3. local

4. mock

Name _____

Author's Purpose

Authors write to **persuade**, **inform**, or **entertain**. How can you find the **author's purpose**? First, look for clues about the genre. Then, ask questions about what you read and find answers.

▶ Answer the questions about *Being a Good Citizen*.

🔍 Page 55 What clues about the genre of this text help you know what type of text you are reading?

_____

_____

_____

_____

🔍 Pages 60–62 What questions were you able to answer about why the author wrote this text? Using all the clues, what do you think is the author's purpose for writing the text?

_____

_____

_____

_____

Name _____

Words to Know

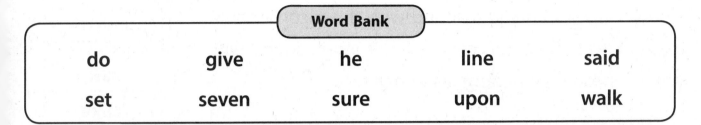

Word Bank				
do	give	he	line	said
set	seven	sure	upon	walk

▶ Circle the word that best completes each sentence.

1. Ben has (seven, set) pets.

2. He likes to (give, walk) with them.

3. They walk in a (sure, line).

4. Ben will (upon, give) them food.

5. (He, Do) will take them to the vet.

6. Ben (sure, set) loves pets!

7. (Do, Said) you love pets?

8. I (said, give), "Yes!"

Long a, i (VCe)

You can spell the long *a* sound with the *a*-consonant-*e* pattern, as in *cake*. You can spell the long *i* sound with the *i*-consonant-*e* pattern, as in *mine*.

▶ Write each basic Spelling Word in the correct column.

Words with long *a*	Words with long *i*
_____	_____
_____	_____
_____	_____
_____	_____
_____	_____

Spelling Words
Basic
cake
mine
plate
size
ate
grape
prize
wipe
race
line
pile
rake
Review
win
flat
rip
if

Name _____

Long a, i (VCe)

The word *gate* has a VCe pattern, vowel-consonant-e. In words with a VCe pattern, the first vowel stands for a long sound, and the final *e* is silent.

▶ Complete each sentence. Use each word from the box once.

Word Bank

| ate | safe | lake | like | time | wade |

1. Dad and Kate walk to the _____ .

2. "I am not sure it is _____ to dive," said Dad.

3. "You can _____ in," Dad said.

4. Kate and Dad _____ a picnic.

5. "It is _____ to go," Dad said.

6. "I _____ to go to the lake," said Kate.

Long a, i (VCe)

You can spell the long *a* sound with the *a*-consonant-*e* pattern, as in *cake*. You can spell the long *i* sound with the *i*-consonant-*e* pattern, as in *mine*.

▶ Read each word. Write the basic or review Spelling Words that rhyme with it.

1. mile　　　_____

2. cape　　　_____

3. chat　　　_____

4. pipe　　　_____

5. face　　　_____

6. flip　　　_____

7. bake　　　_____　　_____

8. gate　　　_____　　_____

9. fine　　　_____　　_____

▶ Which two basic Spelling Words rhyme with *rise*, but are not spelled with *–ise*? Circle them in the list. Write two sentences that use these words.

Spelling Words
Basic
cake
mine
plate
size
ate
grape
prize
wipe
race
line
pile
rake
Review
win
flat
rip
if

Name _____

Power Words: Match

Word Bank

disaster	fiddled	hamper	mood
perfect	planned	queasy	scowl

▶ Write the Power Word from *Picture Day Perfection* that best fits each item.

1. Which word means the opposite of *smile*? _____

2. Which word names a terrible event? _____

3. Which word can mean the opposite of *ruined*? _____

4. You might feel like this when you are sick. _____

5. Which word means almost the same as *prepared*? _____

6. Which word is a place for dirty clothes? _____

7. This word means *jiggled* or *picked at.* _____

8. Which word means *the way you feel*? _____

Name _____

Characters

The **characters** are the people or animals in a story. **External traits** are what we see about them. **Internal traits** are thoughts, words, and feelings.

▶ Answer the questions about *Picture Day Perfection*.

🔍 Pages 73–76 What words would you use to describe the boy? Why did you choose those words?

_____

_____

_____

_____

_____

_____

🔍 Pages 80–81 What is surprising about what happens in this part of the story? What does the boy's reaction tell you about him?

_____

_____

_____

_____

Name _____

Phonics Review

In words with the VC*e* pattern, the first vowel stands for a long vowel sound, and the final *e* is silent. The word *dislike* has two syllables. Blend the CVC syllable and the VC*e* syllable to read the word.

When the vowels *e* or *i* follow *c* and *g*, the letters usually stand for a soft sound, like in *mice* and *cage*.

▶ Read the words in the Word Bank. Write a word to complete each sentence.

Word Bank

advice   cage   dislikes   escape   wise

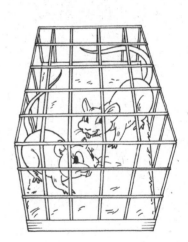

1. Midge and Mom see pet mice in

   a _____ .

2. "Gem the cat _____ mice,"
   said Midge.

3. "If the mice _____ , Gem
   will get them."

4. "It is not _____ to have a cat
   and mice as pets."

5. "Yes," said Mom. "My _____ is
   no mice for us!"

Name _____

Inflections –ed, –ing

Add *–ed* to the end of a **verb** to tell about an action in the past.
Add *–ing* to the end of a verb to tell about an action that is
happening now or that may happen in the future.

▶ Choose the word that best completes each sentence.
Write the word on the line. Circle the word(s) in the sentence
that tell you when the action happened.

1. Last week, I _____ the ball into the goal.

    kicked   **kicking**

2. Tomorrow I will be _____ with friends.

    played   **playing**

3. When I was little, I _____ the ball with my hands.

    rolled   **rolling**

4. Now I am _____ it from knee to knee!

    bounced   **bouncing**

▶ Choose another verb about a sport or a hobby. On the lines,
write the verb in the past, present, and future tense.

5. _____

    _____

Name _____

Words to Know

Knowing how to read and write these words can make you a better reader and writer.

Word Bank

cold	come	close	done	fire
front	life	small	name	times

▶ Fill in the blanks to complete the sentences. Write a word from the box on each line.

1. It sure is _____ !

2. I walk to the _____ to see.

3. I see a _____ cat face!

4. I let the cat _____ in.

5. The cat ate, and I made a _____ .

6. The cat sat _____ at my side.

▶ Write a sentence about what might happen next. Use at least one word from the box.

_____

_____

Name _____

Long o, u (VCe)

You can spell the long *o* sound with the *o*-consonant-*e* pattern, as in *rose*. You can spell the long *u* sound with the *u*-consonant-*e* pattern, as in *tune*.

▶ Write each basic Spelling Word in the correct column.

Words with long *o*	Words with long *u*
_____	_____
_____	_____
_____	_____
_____	_____
_____	_____
_____	_____
_____	_____

Spelling Words
Basic
doze
nose
use
rose
pole
close
June
woke
rule
rode
role
tune
Review
hum
shut
frog
job

Name _____

Long o, e, u (CV, VCe)

The word *no* has a consonant-vowel, or CV pattern.
Words and syllables with a CV pattern end with a long
vowel sound. The word *note* has a vowel-consonant-*e*, or
VC*e* pattern. In words with a VC*e* pattern, the first vowel
stands for a long vowel sound, and the final *e* is silent.

▶ Complete each sentence. Use each word from the box once.

Word Bank					
be	use	huge	no	cute	hole

1. Pete Mole has _____ home.

2. Pete will dig a _____ .

3. He can _____ it as a home.

4. The hole can not _____ small.

5. So Pete makes a _____ hole.

6. It is a _____ home for a mole.

Name _____

Long o, u (VCe)

You can spell the long *o* sound with the *o*-consonant-*e* pattern, as in *nose*. You can spell the long *u* sound with the *u*-consonant-*e* pattern, as in *June*.

▶ Read each sentence. Cross out the Spelling Word that is spelled incorrectly. Write it correctly on the line.

1. Jan will clooz the door when she goes out. _____

2. We sang a happy toone in music class. _____

3. Please put the roze in the vase. _____

4. Our class has a rul about helping others. _____

5. I woak up late for school yesterday. _____

6. The flag waves on the poole. _____

▶ Write five more sentences with Spelling Words. Then trade with a partner and check each other's sentences.

Spelling Words
Basic
doze
nose
use
rose
pole
close
June
woke
rule
rode
role
tune
Review
hum
shut
frog
job

Name _____

Phonics Review

A word with a consonant-vowel, or CV pattern, ends with the long vowel sound. A word with a vowel-consonant-*e*, or VC*e* pattern, has a long vowel sound. The final *e* is silent. The long vowel sounds are the same as the letter names: *a, e, i, o,* and *u.*

▶ Write two words to complete each sentence.

1. I can make _____ with a _____ .

   tub   **tube**   **flute**   **music**

2. The _____ says the bike is

   for _____ .

   label   **lab**   **sale**   **base**

3. _____ can not _____ on a book.

   decide   **me**   **Eve**   **delete**

4. A _____ can _____ in
   a small plane.

   pilot   **glide**   **pile**   **pit**

5. Can you _____ your _____ on a map?

   go   **hope**   **home**   **locate**

Power Words: Match

Word Bank

amount	easily	example	forms
material	planet	space	tasty

▶ Write the Power Word from *Many Kinds of Matter* that best fits each item.

1. Which word describes how you do something that is not too hard?   _____

2. Which word describes Earth?   _____

3. Which word describes your favorite food?   _____

4. Which word describes what something is made from?   _____

5. Which word means almost the same as *an open area*?   _____

6. Which word tells how much there is of something?   _____

7. Which word describes shapes you can see or make?   _____

8. This word is used to explain how one thing is part of a group.   _____

Name _____

Suffixes –er, –est

A **suffix** is a word part added to the end of a base word that changes the meaning of the word. The suffix –er means "more." Add –er to the end of an **adjective**, or describing word, to compare two things. The suffix –est means "most." Add –est to compare three or more things.

▶ Add –er and –est to the base word to make two new words. Write the new words on the lines. Tell a partner what each word means and how you would use it.

1. clean _____   _____

2. nice _____   _____

▶ Choose the word from the box that completes the sentence. Write the word on the line.

```
┌──────────────────( Word Bank )──────────────────┐
│                                                  │
│   bigger        longest        neatest     sweeter │
│                                                  │
└──────────────────────────────────────────────────┘
```

3. That is the _____ piece of string that I have ever seen!

4. My dog is _____ than your puppy.

5. You have the _____ desk in the classroom.

6. I think this apple tastes _____ than that apple.

Content-Area Words

Informational texts often use words from science and social studies to tell about a topic. Readers can use **context clues** to figure out a word's meaning. Context clues are the words and sentences around an unknown word that can be clues to its meaning.

▶ Answer the questions about *Many Kinds of Matter.*

🔍 Pages 104–106   How are all solids the same?

_____

_____

_____

_____

_____

🔍 Pages 114–115   Underline the sentences where *evaporation* and *condensation* are first used. Which word in each sentence is a clue to the meanings of *evaporation* and *condensation*?

_____

_____

_____

_____

Name _____

Synonyms

Synonyms are words that mean the same or almost the same thing. *Happy* and *glad* are examples of synonyms.

Word Bank				
beautiful	dull	little	silent	tune

▶ Read each sentence. Identify the word from the box that means the same or almost the same as the underlined word. Write it on the line.

1. Let's sing a <u>song</u> together. _____

2. It was <u>quiet</u> in the library. _____

3. I thought the movie was <u>boring</u>. _____

4. The flowers in Nell's garden are <u>pretty</u>. _____

5. Do you want to hold this <u>tiny</u> kitten? _____

▶ Choose one of the sentences above. Explain its meaning. Then on the lines below, write new synonyms for the underlined word.

6. _____

_____

Name _____

Select a Topic

Follow these steps to select a topic.

1. Brainstorm topics that interest you.

2. Choose three topics. Pick ones that interest you the most.

3. For each topic, list what you already know. Then select a topic.

▶ **Writing Prompt:** Look outside. What are you most curious about?

1. Brainstorm topics about the prompt.

Possible Topics

1. _____   **4.** _____

2. _____   **5.** _____

3. _____   **6.** _____

2. Choose three topics that interest you the most.

1. _____

2. _____

3. _____

Name _____

3. Write your three topics in the chart below. For each of the topics, list what you already know. Then select a topic.

TOPICS	1.	2.	3.
WHAT I ALREADY KNOW			

My final topic is _____ .

_____

Name _____

Words to Know

Word Bank				
answer	find	its	miss	old
round	then	until	what	young

▶ Fill in the blanks to complete the sentences. Write a word from the box on each line.

1. _____ is in the basket?

2. I need to know the _____ !

3. I cannot wait _____ June comes home.

4. I open the big, _____ basket.

5. There is a _____ rabbit inside!

6. I look at its face, and _____ I pet it.

7. How _____ are you, rabbit?

8. Do you _____ your pals?

9. Let's _____ you kale to bite.

Name _____

Short and Long Vowels (CVC, VCe)

You can spell short vowel sounds with the consonant-vowel-consonant (CVC) pattern, as in *cap*. You can spell long vowel sounds with the vowel-consonant-*e* (VCe) pattern, as in *cape*.

▶ Write each basic Spelling Word in the correct column.

Words with short vowels (CVC)	Words with long vowels (VCe)
_____	_____
_____	_____
_____	_____
_____	_____
_____	_____

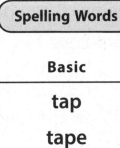

Spelling Words

Basic

tap

tape

fin

fine

cute

ride

rob

robe

cap

cape

slid

slide

Review

shop

wish

cut

rid

Name _____

Short and Long Vowels (CVC, VCe)

The word *cap* has a CVC pattern and a short vowel sound. The word *cape* has a VCe pattern. The final *e* is silent, but it lets you know the first vowel letter stands for a long vowel sound.

▶ Write the words to complete the sentence.

1. What small _____ can _____ get?

   Pete   **pet**

2. I got a _____ to make a _____ .

   kite   **kit**

3. Mel did _____ see the _____ on the pad.

   note   **not**

4. Mom will _____ the van to pick

   _____ up.

   use   **us**

5. Jane will _____ a trip on a _____ .

   plan   **plane**

Name _____

Short and Long Vowels (CVC, VCe)

You can spell short vowel sounds with the consonant-vowel-consonant (CVC) pattern as in *cap*. You can spell long vowel sounds with the vowel-consonant-e (VCe) pattern as in *cape*.

▶ Follow the directions for each item. Write the Spelling Word on the line.

1. Add an *e* to *tap*. _____

2. Drop the *e* in *robe*. _____

3. Add an *e* to *fin*. _____

4. Add an *e* to *cut*. _____

5. Drop the *e* in *cape*. _____

6. Drop the *e* in *slide*. _____

7. Add an *e* to *rid*. _____

8. Drop the *e* in *tape*. _____

▶ Which four Spelling Words did you *not* write? Circle them in the list. Write a sentence for each word.

Spelling Words
Basic
tap
tape
fin
fine
cute
ride
rob
robe
cap
cape
slid
slide
Review
shop
wish
cut
rid

Power Words: Draw and Write

Word Bank

| battleground | feud | frenzy | gasped |

▶ Draw a picture or write words that will help you remember each Power Word from *The Great Fuzz Frenzy*. Try to write more than you draw.

1. battleground

2. feud

3. frenzy

4. gasped

Name _____

Connect Text and Visuals

Visuals can help you understand what the author's words don't say. Illustrations can give you details about the characters, setting, or events in a text. In the same way, the **type**, or printed words, an author uses and where the author places it can show a sequence of events or even which character is talking.

▶ Answer the questions about *The Great Fuzz Frenzy*.

🔍 Page 125 What do you notice about the words *boink,* *thump,* and *rumble* on the left side of the picture? What do these words help you understand?

_____

_____

_____

_____

🔍 Pages 148–149 What happened to Big Bark? Why did this happen? How does the picture help you understand how stealing the fuzz led to this problem?

_____

_____

_____

_____

Name _____

Phonics Review

A syllable with the CVC pattern has a short vowel sound. A syllable with the VCe pattern has a long vowel sound. The syllables –er and –est help us compare people and things.

▶ Read the words in the Word Bank. Write a word to complete each sentence.

Word Bank

| not | smaller | smallest | bike | colder | coldest |

1. Dad has a big _____ .

2. Sam has a _____ bike than Dad.

3. Eve has the _____ bike of all.

4. "It is _____ cold yet," said Dad.

5. "But it will get _____ as we ride up."

6. Eve said, "It will be the _____ at the top!"

Name _____

Inflections -s, -es

The endings –s or –es added to the end of a **noun** make it **plural**, or change the number of something. The endings –s or –es added to the end of a **verb** show that an action is happening now, or in the present.

▶ Add –s or –es to the noun or verb in parentheses. Write the new word on the line to complete the sentence.

1. Cam (walk) _____ to school with her friends.

2. Lin threw two (ball) _____ through the basketball hoop.

3. Max moved the (box) _____ into the closet.

4. Alex (ride) _____ her bike across the street.

5. Emma (ask) _____ her teacher for help.

6. I watched two (movie) _____ on Saturday.

7. She (catch) _____ the ball from the pitcher.

8. The dog (eat) _____ everything in its bowl.

Name _____

Power Words: Yes or No?

> **Word Bank**
>
> plumes   strokes   tumbling   wisps

▶ Read each sentence. Circle **YES** if the word makes sense or **NO** if it does not. Rewrite the sentence so it makes sense.

1. **Plumes** of clouds make long and thin shapes.

   YES   NO

   _____

2. Your friend **strokes** his dog in a nice, gentle way.

   YES   NO

   _____

3. Rocks **tumbling** down a hill are still.

   YES   NO

   _____

   _____

4. **Wisps** of smoke look like big, fluffy clouds.

   YES   NO

   _____

Name _____

Elements of Poetry

Poetry is a special kind of writing. Poems have **rhythm,** visual **patterns**, and descriptive language. Some poems are written in **stanzas**. These things make the poem pleasing to the eye and ear.

▶ Answer the questions about *Water Rolls, Water Rises.*

🔍 Pages 162–163 Compare and contrast the settings on pages 162 and 163. How do the words and phrases that the poet chose create two very different settings?

_____

_____

_____

_____

🔍 Pages 170–171 How are the describing words and phrases on page 170 different from those on page 171?

_____

_____

_____

_____

Name _____

Words to Know

▶ Write the word that best completes each sentence.

1. I see a baby _____ outside.

2. The bird is tan and _____ .

3. It can _____ .

4. It does not sit in one _____ .

5. The bird has a _____ beak.

6. It will _____ a twig to its nest.

7. _____ bird can see Pam.

8. _____ can see it from her window.

Blends with *l, r, s*

You can spell a word with a blend by listening for the sound of each letter in the blend. Some blends include the letters *l, r,* or *s.*

place   drag   swim

▶ Write each basic Spelling Word in the correct column.

Spelling Words
Basic

Blends with *l*	**Blends with *r***	**Blends with *s***	Basic Words
_____	_____	_____	space
_____	_____	_____	globe
_____	_____	_____	grade
_____	_____	_____	swim
_____	_____	_____	place
_____	_____	_____	last
_____	_____	_____	test

Spelling Words

Basic
space
globe
grade
swim
place
last
test
skin
drag
glide
just
stove

Review
slid
close
grape
plate

Name _____

Blends with *l, r, s*

The word *plum* begins with two consonants, or a consonant blend. You say and blend each consonant sound to read the word. The word *strap* begins with three consonants. You say and blend each consonant sound to read the word.

▶ Read the question. Write the word that names the picture.

Is it a **flip, clip, strip**?

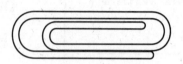

_____

Is it a **grade, glade, blade**?

_____

Is it a **plug, snug, slug**?

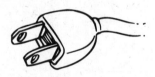

_____

Is it a **throne, stone, scone**?

_____

Is it a **spice, price, slice**?

_____

Is it a **frame, fame, flame**?

_____

Name _____

Blends with *l, r, s*

You can spell a word with a blend by listening for the sound of each letter in the blend. Some blends include the letters *l, r,* or *s.*

  globe   grade   stove

▶ Write the Spelling Word that best completes each sentence.

1. Dad cooked dinner on the _____ .

2. I got a good _____ on my project.

3. See the bird _____ through the air.

4. The slow runner came in _____ .

5. Jane did well on her math _____ .

6. Cal likes to _____ in the pool.

7. He got a sunburn on his _____ .

8. The library has a _____ of the world.

▶ Write four more sentences with missing Spelling Words, like the ones on this page. Trade with a partner. Complete each other's sentences.

Power Words: Match

```
┌─────────────────────  Word Bank  ─────────────────────┐
│                                                        │
│    ace          agency        business      confidently │
│                                                        │
│    eagerly      located       mystery         seeps    │
│                                                        │
└────────────────────────────────────────────────────────┘
```

▶ Write the Power Word from *The Puddle Puzzle* that best fits each item.

1. Which word means the opposite of *pours out*? _____

2. Which word names a place where people work to help others? _____

3. Which word do you use to tell where something is? _____

4. Which word names something that is unknown or hard to understand? _____

5. Which word describes how you act when you feel sure you can do something well? _____

6. Which word describes how you would act if you really wanted to go to the park? _____

7. Which word describes what happens at a place where people shop? _____

8. Which word means *really good*? _____

Name _____

Elements of Drama

A **drama** is a story acted out by people. The parts of a drama include a **cast of characters**, **dialogue**, the **setting**, **scenes**, and **stage directions**.

▶ Answer the questions about *The Puddle Puzzle*.

🔍 Pages 182–183 What is the purpose of the Cast of Characters and Setting? What is the purpose of the dialogue?

_____

_____

_____

_____

_____

_____

🔍 Pages 186–187 Which characters' actions are described with stage directions? What do you learn about them from the stage directions?

_____

_____

_____

_____

Phonics Review

- A blend has two or three consonants together. The sounds blend together. You can hear each sound. The word *grin* has the blend *gr*.

- Add –*s* to most words to show more than one thing. Add –*es* to words that end in *s* or *x* to show more than one thing.

▶ To name each picture, add –*s* or –*es* to the one correct word.

fox   frog   _____

grade   globe   _____

stake   snake   _____

bus   gas   _____

flag   frog   _____

robe   rose   _____

Words That Name Places

Nouns are words that name people, places, and things. Nouns that name places tell where something is happening.

▶ Choose the word from the box that completes the sentence. Write the word on the line.

Word Bank

| closet | home | library | playground | pond | store |

1. Dad will buy milk at the _____ .

2. Dev forgot his gym sneakers at _____ .

3. Tonya saw a big frog near the _____ .

4. We must all be quiet at the _____ .

5. Please hang your coat in the _____ .

6. Tia slid down the slide at the _____ .

▶ Find one of the words above in a dictionary. Write the meaning below.

_____

_____

Name _____

Words to Know

Knowing how to read and write these words can make you a better reader and writer.

Word Bank				
are	hand	kept	king	land
long	sing	thing	think	wish

▶ Circle the word that best completes each sentence.

1. The (king, long) is nice.

2. He rules the (kept, land).

3. The king likes to (thing, sing).

4. He has a cane in his (long, hand).

5. He has a (wish, sing).

6. What do you (kept, think) it is?

▶ Write sentences using two new words from the box.

_____

_____

Name _____

Final Blends

Some consonant blends are at the ends of words. You can spell these words by listening for the sound of each letter in a blend.

end   *long*   *stamp*

▶ Write each basic Spelling Word in the correct box.

Words with *nd*	Words with *mp*
_____	_____
_____	_____
_____	_____

Words with *nk*	Words with *ng*
_____	_____
_____	_____
_____	_____

Words with *xt*	Words with *nt*
_____	_____
_____	_____
_____	_____

Spelling Words

Basic

next
end
camp
sank
sing
drink
hunt
stand
long
stamp
pond
bring

Review

globe
swim
stove
just

Final Blends

The word *last* has the CVCC short vowel pattern. It ends with a consonant blend. In a consonant blend, each letter keeps its own sound, and you say the sounds closely together. In words like *ring* and *rink*, the consonants blend together to make new sounds.

▶ Choose and write two words to complete each sentence.

1. I _____ my _____ by the sink.

rang   ring   left   last

2. The frogs _____ into the _____ .

just   pond   pest   jump

3. Jan _____ to her _____ lesson.

went   wink   trinket   trumpet

4. Frank has a _____ for the _____ trip.

command   camping   tend   tent

5. Who can _____ this _____ ?

task   list   trunk   lift

6. You can get a _____ at the _____ .

bring   sink   sing   drink

Final Blends

Some consonant blends are at the ends of words. You can spell these words by listening for the sound of each letter in a blend.

dri*nk*   si*ng*   po*nd*

▶ Read each clue. Unscramble the word. Write the Spelling Word correctly on the line.

1. Fish swim in this   dpno   _____

2. Do this to songs   isng   _____

3. Not short   lngo   _____

4. Put this on a letter   psmta   _____

5. Do this with a tent   acmp   _____

6. Did not swim   ksna   _____

7. Do not sit   nsatd   _____

8. Do this from a cup   irnkd   _____

9. Stop   dne   _____

▶ Choose other Spelling Words. Make up a clue for each one. Scramble the letters. Ask a partner to write the words correctly.

Spelling Words
Basic
next
end
camp
sank
sing
drink
hunt
stand
long
stamp
pond
bring
Review
globe
swim
stage
must

Phonics Review

- The word *test* has the CVCC short vowel pattern. It ends with a consonant blend. Each letter keeps its own sound. In words like *ring* and *rink*, the consonants blend together to make new sounds.

- If a word has two vowels with two consonants between them, you can divide the word into syllables between the consonants. Blend the syllables to read the word: *con/test = contest.*

▶ Write the word that completes each sentence.

1. I can put the figs in a _____ .

   brink **basket** **bitten**

2. You must use a _____ when you ride a bike.

   happen **hang** **helmet**

3. Our class has a pet _____ in a tank.

   rest **reptile** **random**

4. I made a big _____ on the gift.

   ribbon **rabbit** **rascal**

5. That _____ plant can prick you.

   crust **cactus** **cancel**

Power Words: Match

Word Bank

greedy	invited	musical	plead
scoots	screams	scurries	shove

▶ Write the Power Word from *Big Red Lollipop* that best fits each item.

1. Which word means that you have been asked to come?   _____

2. Which word means *wants more than what is fair*?   _____

3. This word describes a pleasant tune.   _____

4. Which word means a *hard push*?   _____

5. This word is the opposite of *whispers*.   _____

6. Which word describes moving with short, fast steps?   _____

7. Which word is the opposite of *moves slowly*?   _____

8. This word means the same as *beg*.   _____

Name _____

Prefixes un-, re-

The **prefix** *un-* means "to reverse" or "not." The prefix *re-* means "again." Use the meaning of the prefix and the **base word** to figure out the meaning of the new word. If you are not sure about the meaning of a base word, use a dictionary.

▶ Add *un-* or *re-* to each word. Then write the meaning of the new word on the line.

1. _____ sure: _____

2. _____ true: _____

3. _____ read: _____

4. _____ tell: _____

5. _____ lucky: _____

6. _____ write: _____

▶ Choose two of the words you made above. Use each in a sentence to show the correct meaning.

_____

_____

_____

_____

Name _____

Point of View

Point of view describes the way readers see things happen in a story. If a story is told from first-person point of view, a character in the story is the narrator. A story told from third-person point of view has an outside narrator.

▶ Answer the questions about *Big Red Lollipop*.

🔍 Pages 208–210 Who is telling the story? What clue in the first sentence on page 208 helps you know?

_____

_____

_____

🔍 Pages 212–215 Who is telling the story now? Is that the same or different as before? What words did you circle that show Rubina is telling the story?

_____

_____

_____

Context Clues

When you come to a word you do not know, use **context clues** to figure out what it means. Look around the word you do not know for clues about what it means.

▶ Read each sentence. Circle the clues in the sentence that help you know the meaning of the underlined word. Use the pictures for help, too! Then circle the meaning.

1. The <u>eager</u> children jumped up and down with delight.

   excited   **tired**

2. A rabbit sleeps in its <u>burrow</u> deep in the ground.

   cage   **hole**

3. Horses ran around and around the <u>circular</u> track.

   long   **round**

4. A breeze blew through the tall grass in the <u>meadow</u>.

   field   **barn**

5. Please <u>discard</u> your trash in the bin outside.

   lift up   **throw away**

6. Sam felt <u>confident</u> that he did a good job on the test.

   sure   **worried**

Social Communication

During a **social** situation, people use **communication** to exchange ideas with others. **Formal language** is used when following the rules of English. **Informal language** is a style of speaking used with friends and family.

▶ Write two examples for each type of language below.

Formal Language	Informal Language

Name _____

Have a conversation with a friend about *Big Red Lollipop*.
Talk about this question:

Would you like to have Rubina as a friend?
Why or why not?

After your conversation, answer the following questions.

Did you use appropriate volume?	Yes	No	Sometimes
Did you speak clearly?	Yes	No	Sometimes
Did you show interest?	Yes	No	Sometimes
Did you nod as you listened?	Yes	No	Sometimes
Did you ask questions?	Yes	No	Sometimes
Did you face your partner?	Yes	No	Sometimes
What language did you use?	Formal	Informal	

What rule do you need to practice more?

_____

_____

Name _____

Words to Know

▶ Write the word that best completes each sentence.
Not all words will be used.

1. Pam drives her _____ .

2. The car is _____ of gas.

3. Pam hikes by the _____ .

4. Pam sees Cal _____ the lane.

5. Cal _____ a rock in
   his hand.

6. A log _____ down in
   the lane.

7. Pam and Cal _____ and pull
   the log.

▶ Write a sentence for a word you did not use yet.

_____

_____

Word Bank

across

car

down

fell

full

held

mountain

pull

push

spell

Name _____

Double Final Consonants

Some short vowel words end with two, or double, consonants that stand for one sound. For example, the letters *ss* in *dress* stand for one sound, /s/.

▶ Write each basic Spelling Word in the correct box.

Words with *ll*

_____
_____
_____
_____
_____

Words with *ss*

_____
_____
_____
_____

Words with *dd*

_____
_____
_____
_____

Words with *ff*

_____
_____
_____
_____

Spelling Words

Basic

full
dress
mess
add
hill
pull
spill
class
doll
kiss
fell
off

Review

drink
stamp
swim
place

Name _____

Double Final Consonants

The word *hill* ends with **double final consonants**. The two consonants stand for one sound.

▶ Read the question and look at the picture. Write the word that names the picture.

Is it **dill** or a **doll**?

_____

Is it a **mitt** or a **mutt**?

_____

Is it **glass** or **grass**?

_____

Is it a **drill** or a **grill**?

_____

Does it **buzz** or **fizz**?

_____

Will we see **liftoff** or **spinoff**?

_____

Name _____

Double Final Consonants

Some short vowel words end with two, or double, consonants that stand for one sound. For example, the letters *ll* in *doll* stand for one sound, /l/.

▶ Write the Spelling Word that best completes each sentence.

1. Jen has a red _____.

2. Bob will _____ on the rope.

3. Do not make a _____.

4. We _____ in math.

5. I am in Miss Rand's _____.

6. Turn the lamp _____.

7. Do not _____ your milk.

8. Mom gave me a hug and a _____.

▶ Write four more sentences with missing Spelling Words, like the ones on this page. Trade with a partner. Complete each other's sentences.

Spelling Words
Basic
full
dress
mess
add
hill
pull
spill
class
doll
kiss
fell
off
Review
drink
stamp
swim
place

Name _____

Power Words: Yes or No?

Word Bank			
argue	blamed	practice	respectful

▶ Read each sentence. Circle **YES** if the word makes sense or **NO** if it does not. Rewrite the sentence so it makes sense.

1. You don't need to **practice** if you want to play the flute well.

        YES   NO

_____

_____

2. You may **argue** with someone if they **blamed** you for doing something wrong.

        YES   NO

_____

_____

3. "Thank you" are **respectful** words that you can say to someone.

        YES   NO

_____

_____

Name _____

Central Idea

The **topic** of a text is the person or thing that text is mostly about. The **central idea** is the most important idea about the topic. Readers can use **supporting evidence,** or details, to identify the central idea.

▶ Answer the questions about *Working with Others*.

🔍 Page 233 What is the main topic of the first paragraph? Which details on this page support the central idea?

_____

_____

_____

_____

_____

🔍 Pages 235–238 What is the central idea of this text? Which details support the central idea?

_____

_____

_____

_____

_____

Name _____

Phonics Review

- In words that end with **double final consonants**, the two consonants stand for one sound. Add *ed* or *ing* to show when an action happens—*spell, spelled, spelling.*

- If a word has a long vowel VC*e* pattern, drop the final *e* and then add *ed* or *ing*—*hike, hiked, hiking.*

- If a word has a short vowel CVC pattern, double the final consonant and then add *ed* or *ing*—*jog, jogged, jogging.*

▶ Write the word that names the action in the picture.

Add **ed** to **spill**. _____ 	Add **ing** to **drive**. _____ 
Add **ed** to **race**. _____ 	Add **ing** to **sniff**. _____ 
Add **ing** to **mop**. _____	Add **ing** to **bat**. _____ 

Inflections –ed, –ing

Add –ed to the end of a **verb** to tell about an action in the past. Add –ing to the end of a verb to tell about an action that is happening in the present or that may happen in the future.

▶ Add –ed and –ing to each verb. Then complete the sentence with the verb that fits.

1. cook   _____   _____

     Long ago, Grandma _____ all of my meals.

2. bake   _____   _____

     Now we are _____ bread together.

3. help   _____   _____

     Grandma _____ me roll the dough.

4. shape   _____   _____

     Now I am _____ the dough.

5. wait   _____   _____

     We will be _____ for the bread to be ready.

▶ Think of a verb that tells about something you like to do at home. Use the word in a sentence that tells about the past.

_____

Name _____

Power Words: Draw and Write

Word Bank			
booming	persuade	skill	threatening

▶ Draw a picture or write words that will help you remember each Power Word from *Gingerbread for Liberty!* Try to write more than you draw.

1. booming

2. persuade

3. skill

4. threatening

Name _____

Text Organization

Text organization is the way a text is arranged to help readers understand the information. Most texts that tell about a person's life are arranged in **chronological order**. This is the order in which events happened.

▶ Answer the questions about *Gingerbread for Liberty*.

🔍 Pages 246–248 What events happen on pages 246–248? How are these events connected? How are the events organized, and why do you think the author organized the events this way?

_____

_____

_____

_____

🔍 Pages 254–259 In your own words, tell what happens in this part of the text. How does the way the text is organized support the author's purpose for writing it?

_____

_____

_____

_____

Name _____

Words to Know

Word Bank

even	mouse	Mr.	Mrs.	other
shall	these	when	while	white

▶ Read the clues. Write the word from the Word Bank that goes with each clue.

1. A man   _____

2. Asks or tells about time   _____

3. A pale color   _____

4. Like a rat   _____

5. For a time, during   _____

6. 2, 4, 6, 8, 10   _____

7. A wife   _____

8. Not this bus, but the   _____

▶ Write a sentence for each word you did not write yet.

_____

_____

Name _____

Consonant Digraphs

You can spell the /sh/ sound with *sh*, as in *push*.
You can spell the /th/ sound with *th*, as in *thin*.
You can spell the /ch/ sound with *ch*, as in *chest*.
You can spell the /hw/ sound with *wh*, as in *white*.

▶ Write each basic Spelling Word in the correct box.

Words with *sh*	Words with *th*
_____	_____
_____	_____
_____	_____
_____	_____

Words with *ch*	Words with *wh*
_____	_____
_____	_____
_____	_____

Spelling Words
Basic
dish
than
chest
such
thin
push
shine
chase
white
while
these
flash
Review
dress
add
off
fell

Name _____

Consonant Digraphs

The word *chop* begins with the **consonant digraph** *ch*. In a digraph, two letters together stand for one sound. Sometimes, three letters together stand for one sound, like the letters *tch* in *match*.

▶ Write two words to complete each sentence.

1. Mrs. Chan went to the fabric _____ to buy _____ .

   dolphin   shop   when   cloth

2. She _____ a soft _____ fabric.

   white   chose   think   crash

3. Mrs. Chan _____ the man and gave him _____ .

   fifth   whim   cash   thanked

4. She cut and _____ the fabric to make six _____ .

   stitched   sashes   this   graph

5. She gave _____ to her class so they will _____ .

   children   with   match   them

6. Her class was _____ and posed for a _____ .

   while   much   photo   thrilled

Name _____

Consonant Digraphs

You can spell the /sh/ sound with *sh,* as in *dish.*
You can spell the /th/ sound with *th,* as in *than.*
You can spell the /ch/ sound with *ch,* as in *chase.*
You can spell the /hw/ sound with *wh,* as in *while.*

▶ Write the missing letters in each Spelling Word.
Then write the Spelling Word on the line.

1. fla_____

   _____

2. _____ile

   _____

3. _____ase

   _____

4. pu_____

   _____

5. su_____

   _____

6. _____an

   _____

7. _____ese

   _____

8. _____ite

   _____

9. _____ine

   _____

10. _____est

   _____

▶ Which two Spelling Words did you *not* write? Circle
them in the list. Write a sentence for each word.

Spelling Words
Basic
dish
than
chest
such
thin
push
shine
chase
white
while
these
flash
Review
dress
add
off
fell

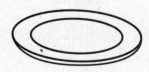

Name _____

Power Words: Match

Word Bank

dragged	excuses	frown	hesitant
mumbled	nearby	wrinkled	yanked

▶ Write the Power Word from *Pepita and the Bully* that best fits each item.

1. Which word means the opposite of *far away?* _____

2. You might act like this when you feel unsure. _____

3. If you did not speak loudly, you spoke like this. _____

4. Which word means the opposite of *smooth?* _____

5. Which word tells how you moved something? _____

6. You might give these for not doing something. _____

7. Which word means *pulled at hard and fast?* _____

8. Which word is the opposite of *smile?* _____

Name _____

Theme

Theme is the **moral**, or lesson, that readers learn from the story. Use these steps to identify the theme: Think about the story's **topic**. Look for the lesson a character learns. Use clues to figure out the message. Explain the theme in your own words.

▶ Answer the questions about *Pepita and the Bully*.

🔍 Pages 268–270 What is this story mostly about? What details in this part of the story help you identify the topic?

_____

_____

_____

🔍 Pages 279–282 What does Pepita realize after she says something mean to Babette? How does this affect the way she tells Babette how she feels about her being a bully? What theme, or lesson, do these details help you figure out?

_____

_____

_____

_____

_____

Name _____

Phonics Review

The word *shop* begins with the **consonant digraph** *sh*. In a digraph, two letters together stand for one sound.

A **prefix** is a word part added to the beginning of a word. The prefix *re–* means "again." The prefix *un–* means "not, or opposite of."

▶ Choose a word from the box to complete each sentence.

Word Bank

| unhitch | unshell | reship | unplug | rethink | unsafe |

1. Mr. Phillips must _____ a box. The last box got smashed.

2. Ask Shane to _____ the ox from the wagon.

3. Riding a bike with no helmet is _____ .

4. Mrs. Chaps had to _____ the nuts to munch on them.

5. Will a bad day make Mitch _____ his plans for a picnic?

6. Mrs. Ash will lift the plug to _____ the sink.

Name _____

Words About Communication

Words about **communication** tell how we share ideas and information. Sometimes we communicate in words. Sometimes we communicate with our faces or bodies. Use a dictionary to look up words you don't know.

▶ Draw a line from the communication words to the correct picture.

1. delighted

2. pleased

Word Bank

giggle   grin   nod

▶ Complete each sentence with the best word from the box.

3. When I meet someone for the first time, I greet them with a

   big _____ .

4. I _____ at my friend when I agree with what she says.

5. My friend knows that I think his joke is funny because

   I _____ .

Name _____

Words to Know

Learn these words. You will see them in your reading and use them in your writing.

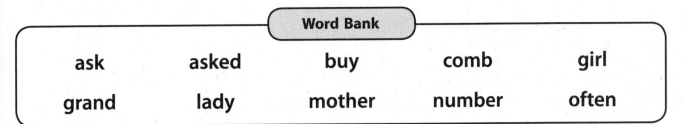

Word Bank

ask	asked	buy	comb	girl
grand	lady	mother	number	often

▶ Fill in the blanks to complete the sentences. Write a word from the box on each line.

1. Kim is a little _____ .

2. She wants a _____ .

3. She will _____ her mom for one.

4. Her _____ said, "Yes."

5. Her mother will _____ it.

6. Kim will use it _____ .

▶ Write a sentence about what might happen next. Use at least one word from the box.

_____

_____

Name _____

Consonants *k*, *ck*

You can spell the /k/ sound with *k*, as in *desk* or *lake*, or with *ck*, as in *rock*.

▶ Write each basic Spelling Word in the correct column.

Words with **ck**	Words with **ke**	Words with **k**
_____	_____	_____
_____	_____	_____
_____	_____	_____
_____	_____	_____
_____	_____	_____
_____	_____	_____

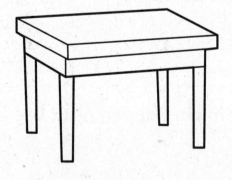

Spelling Words

Basic

milk

neck

ask

snake

truck

kick

smoke

rock

desk

black

lake

trick

Review

dish

white

such

flash

Name _____

Consonants *k*, *ck*

The word *kick* begins with the consonant letter *k*. It ends with the consonant letters *ck*. The consonants *k* and *ck* stand for the same sound.

▶ Write two words to complete each sentence.

1. A _____ and a

   _____ are birds.

   skunk   duck   gecko   chicken

2. They _____ in the grass and mud with

   _____ .

   kept   peck   skill   rocket

3. They _____ on insects, like ants and

   _____ .

   snack   baking   restock   crickets

4. They make nests with small _____ and

   _____ grass.

   flakes   thick   sticks   blocks

5. Moms sit on eggs until the _____ and

   _____ hatch.

   checks   chicks   ducked   ducklings

Name _____

Consonants k, ck

You can spell the /k/ sound with *k*, as in *ask* or *smoke*, or with *ck*, as in *truck*.

▶ Read each sentence. Cross out the Spelling Word that is spelled incorrectly. Write it correctly on the line.

1. Dad drives a yellow truk.   _____

2. We swam in the lacke.   _____

3. The teacher sat at her desc.   _____

4. The frog sat on the rok.   _____

5. The snace is in the grass.   _____

6. Kik the ball to me.   _____

7. The car is blak.   _____

8. I put milck in my glass.   _____

9. The fire made lots of smock.   _____

▶ Write three sentences with the basic Spelling Words you did not use. Then trade with a partner. Check each other's spelling.

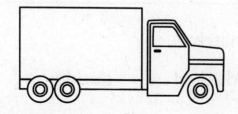

94

Spelling Words

Basic

milk

neck

ask

snake

truck

kick

smoke

rock

desk

black

lake

trick

Review

dish

white

such

flash

Name _____

Phonics Review

- In the word *kick*, the letters *k* and *ck* both stand for the same sound.

- The *k* is silent in the word *knit*. The letters *wr, gn,* and *mb* also have a silent letter.

▶ Write the word that names the picture.

knife **knock**	**snack** **snake**

_____	_____
sing **sign**	**gnome** **gnash**
_____	_____
thumbprint **thumbtack**	**kickstand** **thumbtack**

_____	_____

Name _____

Power Words: Match

Word Bank

clue	cozy	disturb	pause
rattled	sense	steaming	tackled

▶ Write the Power Word from *How to Read a Story* that best fits each item.

1. Which word describes a place that
is warm and nice to be?   _____

2. This word means the same
as *hint*.   _____

3. Which word means *to stop doing
something for a short time*?   _____

4. Which word means *easy to
understand*?   _____

5. This word means the same as
pushed to the ground.   _____

6. Which word means the same as
bother?   _____

7. This word can be used to describe a
hot bowl of soup.   _____

8. Which word is an action that
creates noise?   _____

Name _____

Suffixes -*ful*, -*less*

A **suffix** is a word part added to the end of a base word that changes the word's meaning. The suffix -*ful* means "full of." The suffix -*less* means "without." Use a dictionary to find the meaning for base words that you do not know.

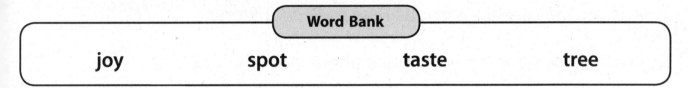

Word Bank			
joy	spot	taste	tree

▶ Read each underlined phrase. Add the suffix -*ful* or -*less* to a word in the box to make a new word that matches the phrase.

1. On my birthday, I am <u>full of joy</u>.   _____

2. My cheese sandwich was <u>without taste</u>.   _____

3. Mason's clean room looked as if it were <u>without a spot</u>.   _____

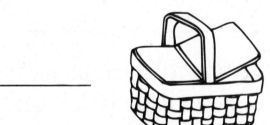

4. We picnicked in an area that was <u>without trees</u>.   _____

▶ Write a sentence for each word.

5. useful   _____

6. useless   _____

Name _____

Text Organization

Authors organize texts to fit the topic and their purpose for writing.
One way to organize texts is **chronological order**, or in the
order instructions should be followed. A **procedural text** gives
instructions for how to do something in chronological order.

▶ Answer the questions about *How to Read a Story*.

🔍 Pages 11–15 What do you notice about how the book is
organized? How does the organization help you understand
why the author wrote the book?

_____

_____

_____

_____

_____

🔍 Pages 18–21 Why do you think the author does not
include a heading with each numbered step?

_____

_____

_____

_____

Multiple-Meaning Words

Multiple-meaning words, or **homographs,** have more than one meaning. You can use **context clues** to figure out the correct meaning.

Word Bank

park   slide   swing   time

▶ Read the story. Complete the sentence with a multiple-meaning word from the box. Underline words in the sentence that helped you know which word to use. Words from the box will be used more than once.

My favorite thing to do with Grandpa is go to the

_____ to play. Grandpa will _____ his car and

then we will walk to the playground. First, Grandpa pushes me

on the _____ . As I _____ higher and higher,

I feel like I can touch the sky. Next, I climb up to the top of the

_____ . I _____ down it really fast and

Grandpa catches me. Finally, it is _____ to

go home. Grandpa and I always have a wonderful

_____ playing together!

Name _____

Give and Follow Instructions

Instructions are directions for how to do something. You should give instructions one step at a time. Use **sequence** words like *first,* *next,* and *last* to help explain the order of steps.

▶ Write instructions below for how to choose a story to read. Make sure to use sequence words to explain the order.

_____

_____

_____

_____

_____

_____

_____

_____

_____

_____

_____

Name _____

Give instructions to a partner about your topic:

How to Choose a Story.

After you give instructions, answer the following questions.

Did you speak clearly?	Yes	No	Sometimes
Did you give instructions one step at a time?	Yes	No	Sometimes
Did you tell the steps in order?	Yes	No	Sometimes
Did you use sequence words like *first* and *last*?	Yes	No	Sometimes
Did you repeat the instructions?	Yes	No	Sometimes

Now listen to a partner give instructions about the same topic.

After you listen to instructions, answer the following questions.

Did you listen carefully?	Yes	No	Sometimes
Did you make eye contact?	Yes	No	Sometimes
Did you listen for sequence words?	Yes	No	Sometimes
Did you ask questions if you needed to?	Yes	No	Sometimes
Did you repeat the instructions?	Yes	No	Sometimes

What rule do you need to practice more?

_____

_____

Name _____

Words to Know

▶ Write the word that best completes each sentence.

1. Meg will _____ the swing.

2. Meg is not _____ .

3. Meg _____ likes to swing.

4. Ron _____ by Meg.

5. "I really like swings, too," Ron _____ .

6. "Let's _____ and swing," Meg says.

7. "_____ swing do you like best?"
   Ron asks.

8. "I _____ pick the blue swing,"
   Meg says.

9. Meg and Ron have a _____ time.

10. "We can swing _____ time!" Ron says.

Word Bank
afraid
always
another
great
passed
really
says
stay
try
which

Name _____

Long a (ai, ay)

You can spell long *a* with *ay*, as in *pay*, or with *ai*, as in *pail*.

▶ Write each basic Spelling Word in the correct column.

Words with *ay*	Words with *ai*
_____	_____
_____	_____
_____	_____
_____	_____
_____	_____

Spelling Words

Basic

pay

wait

paint

train

pail

clay

tray

plain

stain

hay

gray

away

Review

lake

snake

black

ask

Name _____

Long a Patterns

The words *day* and *rain* have the long *a* vowel teams, *ay* and *ai*. The letter *a* can also stand for long *a* in open syllables in words like *basin*.

▶ Write two words to complete each sentence.

1. Gramps and Gail _____ plans to go ice _____ .

   main   made   skating   staining

2. They had to _____ a _____ ride to the rink.

   stay   waist   take   subway

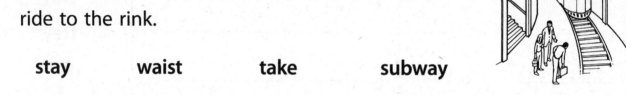

3. At the rink, Gramps _____ to rent ice _____ .

   paid   play   skates   slates

4. Gail _____ up her skates as she _____ for him.

   waited   laced   wayside   laying

5. "This is going to be a fun _____ !" Gail _____ .

   day   laid   relay   exclaims

Name _____

Long a (ai, ay)

You can spell long *a* with *ay*, as in *hay*, or with *ai*, as in *train*.

▶ Write the Spelling Word that best completes each sentence.

1. _____ the fence white.

2. The jam made a _____ on my dress.

3. The sky is _____ on rainy days.

4. _____ for me!

5. We took the _____ to go to the lake.

6. Fill the _____ with sand.

7. Put your socks _____.

8. We stand in line to _____ for lunch.

▶ Write four more sentences with missing Spelling Words, like the ones on this page. Then trade with a partner. Complete each other's sentences.

Spelling Words
Basic
pay
wait
paint
train
pail
clay
tray
plain
stain
hay
gray
away
Review
lake
snake
black
ask

Name _____

Power Words: Draw and Write

Word Bank

| bind | clever | narrow | plain |

▶ Draw a picture or write words that will help you remember each Power Word from *A Crow, a Lion, and a Mouse! Oh, My!* Try to write more than you draw.

1. clever

2. plain

3. narrow

4. bind

Name _____

Elements of Drama

A **drama** is a story acted out by people. The parts of a drama include a **cast of characters, dialogue,** the **setting, scenes,** and **stage directions.**

▶ Answer the questions about *A Crow, A Lion, and a Mouse! Oh, My!*

🔍 Pages 32–33 What do the stage directions tell you?

_____

_____

_____

🔍 Page 34 Find details in the dialogue that explain how Crow 1 and Crow 2 are different. How are their perspectives about the pitcher different? How does the setting help you understand what is happening?

_____

_____

_____

_____

_____

_____

Name _____

Phonics Review

The word *cape* has the VCe pattern for long *a*. The words *rain* and *day* have the vowel teams *ai* and *ay* for long *a*. The letter *a* can also stand for the long *a* sound in open syllables in words like *bacon*. For long words, read one syllable at a time. Use vowel patterns.

▶ Read the clues. Write the word that answers the clue.

1. I tell how a scraped leg feels. _____

   payment   **painful**   **repaint**

2. I name a place in some homes. _____

   basement   **blockade**   **bakeshop**

3. I name a pile of dry grasses. _____

   hilltop   **hailing**   **haystack**

4. I am another name for a dog. _____

   canine   **complain**   **crayon**

5. I name a thing you can eat. _____

   basic   **bagel**   **basin**

6. I name a place for trains. _____

   retrace   **railway**   **raindrops**

Name _____

Words That Describe People, Places, Things

Adjectives are describing words. They can tell how things look, sound, smell, feel, or taste. They may also tell what a person or thing is like or how they act. If you see an adjective that you do not know, look up the word in the dictionary.

▶ Write words that describe each picture on the lines below. Use a dictionary to help you find interesting adjectives.

1.   sight   sound   touch   act/is like

   _____   _____   _____   _____

2.   sight   smell   touch   taste

   _____   _____   _____   _____

3.   sight   is like   smell   touch

   _____   _____   _____   _____

4.   sight   sound   smell   touch

   _____   _____   _____   _____

5.   sight   sound   touch   act/is like

   _____   _____   _____   _____

109

Power Words: Yes or No?

Word Bank

| believe | fulfill | journey | speech |

▶ Read each sentence. Circle **YES** if the word makes sense or **NO** if it does not. Rewrite the sentence so it makes sense.

1. If you *believe* something, you think that it is true.

      YES   NO

_____

2. When you *fulfill* a task, you do not finish it.

      YES   NO

_____

3. We went on a *journey* from our school to the science museum.

      YES   NO

_____

4. When you give a *speech,* you only talk to yourself.

      YES   NO

_____

Name _____

Figurative Language

Literal language uses words that mean exactly what they say.
Figurative language uses words that mean something different
from what they say. Two types of figurative language are:

- **simile:** compares two different things using the word *like* or *as*

- **idiom:** words that mean something different from their everyday
  meaning

▶ Answer the questions about *Hollywood Chicken*.

🔍 Page 45 Luz tells Chicken Lily that she knows "you will
knock their socks off." Is this literal language? Explain why or
why not. How might Luz say what she means in a literal way?

_____

_____

_____

_____

🔍 Pages 46–47 On page 46, what does Chicken Lily compare
herself to when answering Luz? Why does she do this?

_____

_____

_____

_____

Name _____

Words to Know

> **Word Bank**
>
> | clean | feel | ground | horse | leave |
> |-------|------|--------|-------|-------|
> | need | please | queen | seen | tree |

▶ Circle the word that best completes each sentence.

1. Todd has a (horse, ground).

2. He makes sure she is (need, clean).

3. Todd will (need, leave) to brush her.

4. Then she will (please, feel) clean.

5. I have (seen, queen) the horse.

6. She is by the (leave, tree).

7. The horse sleeps on the (ground, clean).

8. May I pet her, (need, please)?

Name _____

Long e (ee, ea)

You can spell long *e* with *ee*, as in *wheel*, or *ea*, as in *each*.

▶ Write each basic Spelling Word in the correct column.

Words with *ee*	Words with *ea*
_____	_____
_____	_____
_____	_____
_____	_____
_____	_____
_____	_____

Spelling Words

Basic

free

teach

teeth

please

each

wheel

team

speak

sneeze

sheep

meaning

weave

Review

away

stain

train

plain

Name _____

Long e, Short e Patterns

The long *e* sound has different spellings. The word *these* has the VC*e* pattern for long *e*. The words *beat* and *meet* have long *e* vowel teams, *ea* and *ee*. The letters *e* and *y* can also stand for long *e* in open syllables in words like *lady* and *she*. The vowel team *ea* can also stand for short *e* in words like *head*.

▶ Write the word that names the picture. Circle the letter or letters that stand for the long *e* sound.

bees belly beads	**treat teeth threat**

_____	_____
secret seated sleeting	**sleepy steamy stampede**

_____	_____
teams thread three	**belly belong baby**

_____	_____

Name _____

Long e (ee, ea)

You can spell long *e* with *ee*, as in *sheep*, or *ea*, as in *weave*.

▶ Read each word. Write the basic Spelling Word that rhymes with it.

1. reach _____ _____

2. leave _____ _____

3. peel _____ _____

4. sneak _____ _____

5. dream _____ _____

6. see _____ _____

7. peep _____ _____

8. cleaning _____ _____

9. freeze _____ _____

10. leak _____ _____

▶ Which word did you not use? Write a sentence for it.

Spelling Words
Basic
free
teach
teeth
please
each
wheel
team
speak
sneeze
sheep
meaning
weave
Review
away
stain
train
plain

Power Words: Match

> **Word Bank**
>
> beamed   chore   dashed   hobbled
>
> jealous   pleasure   superb   thrilled

▶ Write the Power Word from *If the Shoe Fits: Two Cinderella Stories* that best fits each item.

1. Which word means the opposite of *the very worst*? _____

2. Which word names a feeling of great joy or happiness? _____

3. If you were in a hurry to get somewhere, you did this. _____

4. Which word names a task that someone must do? _____

5. Which word is the opposite of *frowned*? _____

6. Which word is the opposite of *feeling glad for someone*? _____

7. Which word means *walked in a slow and uneven way*? _____

8. Which word describes feeling excited? _____

Name _____

Story Structure

Most stories have the same **story structure**. In the beginning, characters face a **conflict**, or problem. The middle of a story has **events** that happen as characters try to solve the conflict. The events at the end explain the **resolution**, or how the conflict is solved. The conflict, events, and resolution make up the story's **plot**.

▶ Answer the questions about *If the Shoe Fits: Two Cinderella Stories*.

🔍 Pages 61–63 What is the conflict Zoey has? Describe how the conflict is resolved and how the story ends.

_____

_____

_____

_____

🔍 Pages 64–68 Retell the main events of the story. What happens at the beginning? What happens in the middle? What happens at the end?

_____

_____

_____

_____

_____

Name _____

Phonics Review

The word *eve* has the VC*e* pattern for long *e*. The words *meat* and *feet* have long *e* vowel teams, *ea* and *ee*. The letters *e* and *y* can also stand for long *e* in open syllables in words like *baby* and *we*. The vowel team *ea* can also stand for short *e* in words like *head*.

Read longer words one syllable at a time. Use the vowel patterns.

► Write a word in each blank to complete the sentences.

1. Zeke is the _____ in the tank top.

   greed   green   deleted   athlete

2. He is running with _____ .

   speed   sunny   treat   speak

3. Zeke _____ in the _____ .

   leak   lead   remains   remakes

4. His _____ clap and _____ for him.

   stream   scream   wealthy   teammates

5. Zeke is _____ that he is _____
   of the others.

   wealthy   happy   ahead   evening

Name _____

Words That Describe Actions

Verbs are words that **describe actions**. They tell exactly what someone or something is doing.

Word Bank

giggled	pushed	sleeps
tumbled	turned	wiped

▶ Complete each sentence using an action word from the box. Use a dictionary if you need help.

1. My cat _____ next to me at night.

2. The large rock _____ down the grassy hill.

3. Mateo _____ at my silly jokes.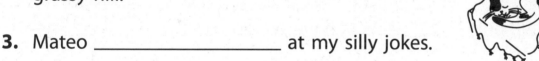

4. Tina _____ the mud off her boots.

5. Chen _____ his little brother on the swing.

6. I _____ around when George tapped my shoulder.

▶ Write a sentence using a verb from the Word Bank.

_____

_____

Name _____

Words to Know

Learn these words. You will see them in your reading and use them in your writing.

> **Word Bank**
>
> below   both   follow   most   move
>
> own   road   show   window   yellow

▶ Read the clues. Write the word from the Word Bank that goes with each clue.

1. The sun is this.   _____

2. Let's run, jump, and _____ !   _____

3. Not all, but _____ insects have wings.   _____

4. A car rides on this.   _____

5. You can look out of this.   _____

6. _____ the line.   _____

7. You can see this on TV.   _____

▶ Write a sentence for a word you did not write yet.

_____

_____

Name _____

Long o (o, oa, ow)

You can spell the /ō/ sound with *o*, as in *most*, *oa*, as in *goat*, or *ow*, as in *own*.

▶ Write each basic Spelling Word in the correct column.

Words with o	Words with oa	Words with ow
_____	_____	_____
_____	_____	_____
_____	_____	_____
_____	_____	_____
_____	_____	_____

Spelling Words

Basic

own

most

soap

float

both

know

loan

goat

flow

loaf

throw

roast

Review

free

speak

sneeze

prize

Name _____

Long o Patterns

The long *o* sound has different spellings. The word *nose* has the VC*e* pattern for long *o*. The words *boat*, *row*, and *toe* have long *o* vowel teams, *oa*, *ow*, *oe*. The letter *o* can also spell long *o* in open syllables as in *donut*, and in words that break the closed syllable rule, as in *both*.

▶ Choose and write two words to complete each sentence.

1. Joan _____ in the _____ .

   stove   mellow   meadow   strolled

2. She spotted an _____ _____ by the trees.

   old   oak   doe   doze

3. A _____ _____ in the tall grass.

   crowed   toast   croaked   toad

4. A _____ _____ up its head.

   mole   posted   mow   poked

5. Joan snapped _____ with her _____ .

   follow   photos   phone   pillow

Name _____

Long o (o, oa, ow)

You can spell the /ō/ sound with *o*, as in *both*, *oa*, as in *loaf*, or *ow*, as in *throw*.

▶ Read each sentence. Cross out the Spelling Word that is spelled incorrectly. Write it correctly on the line.

1. Mom made rost beef. _____

2. Use sope to wash the dishes. _____

3. Who made the moast goals? _____

4. Thro the ball to me. _____

5. We can milk a gowt. _____

6. Do you knoe the answer? _____

7. I can flote on my back. _____

8. I oan that pen. _____

9. We can bowth fit on the seat. _____

▶ Write three sentences with the basic Spelling Words you did not use. Then trade with a partner. Check each other's spelling.

Spelling Words
Basic
own
most
soap
float
both
know
loan
goat
flow
loaf
throw
roast
Review
free
speak
sneeze
prize

Phonics Review

There are many spellings for long *o*. The word *rose* has the VC*e* pattern for long *o*. The words *float*, *know*, and *doe* have long *o* vowel teams, *oa*, *ow*, *oe*. The letter *o* can also spell long *o* in open syllables as in *bonus*, and in words that break the closed syllable rule, as in *most*.

▶ Choose and write the word that answers each riddle.

1. What can roll up and down on a string? _____

   yolk   **yellow**   **yo-yo**   **yodel**

2. What can be a home away from home? _____

   hotel   **hello**   **hippo**   **hollow**

3. What can swim in a glass bowl? _____

   glowing   **growth**   **groan**   **goldfish**

4. What can you make outside in the cold? _____

   snowing   **snowflake**   **snowman**   **snowstorm**

5. What can follow you on sunny days? _____

   stroke   **scroll**   **shadow**   **showing**

Power Words: Match

assured	contraption	exactly	intent
peered	precise	replica	respond

▶ Write the Power Word from *Going Places* that best fits each item.

1. Which word could you use to
   describe an exact measurement?   _____

2. Which word means the same as
   promised?   _____

3. You may call a strange-looking
   object by this name.   _____

4. Which word means something is a
   perfect copy of something else?   _____

5. This word describes you when you
   won't give up on a task.   _____

6. Which word means *looked at
   something closely*?   _____

7. Which word is an adverb that
   means *in every way*?   _____

8. This is what you do when someone
   asks a question.   _____

Name _____

Suffixes –y, –ly

A **suffix** is a word part added to the end of a base word that
changes the meaning of the word. The suffix –y means "having or
being like something" and changes the base word to an **adjective**.
The suffix –ly means "how" or "when" and changes the base word
to an **adverb**.

Word Bank

| bumpy | carefully | rocky |
| springy | weekly | |

▶ Complete each sentence with a word from the box.
Circle *adjective* or *adverb* to tell what kind of word it is.

1. This path uphill is very _____ .   adjective   adverb

2. We must climb up _____ .   adjective   adverb

3. The moss feels _____ under   adjective   adverb
   my feet.

4. The rock feels very _____ .   adjective   adverb

5. We plan a new hike _____ .   adjective   adverb

▶ Add –y or –ly to each word and write the meaning for the
new word.

6. fierce _____ means _____

7. itch _____ means _____

Character

The **characters** in a story are the people or animals whom the story is about. We learn about characters by looking for clues about their traits. **External traits** tell how a character looks. **Internal traits** describe a character's personality.

▶ Answer the questions about *Going Places*.

🔍 Pages 89–91 What is Rafael doing on page 89? How does this help you get to know what he is like? How does Rafael feel in this part of the story and why? Why does he feel this way?

_____

_____

_____

_____

_____

🔍 Pages 92–94 What words would you use to describe Maya and why? How is Maya's perspective different from Rafael's?

_____

_____

_____

_____

Name _____

Reference Sources

When you read, you may see a word that you do not know. Use a **dictionary** or a **glossary** to find out what the word means and how to pronounce it. Remember that the words in a dictionary or a glossary are listed in **alphabetical order**.

▶ Write the words in alphabetical order.

> **1.** rough, munch, might
>
> _____

> **2.** bellow, cool, bounced
>
> _____

▶ Pick two words used above to look up in a dictionary. Pronounce the words. Then write what the words mean.

3. _____

_____

4. _____

_____

Name _____

Recount an Experience

When you **recount** an **experience**, you tell about something that happened to you. Stay on topic. Speak loudly and clearly in complete sentences. Tell about events in order. Share details and facts that will interest your listeners. Then be prepared to answer questions.

▶ Read one child's recounting of the race in *Going Places*. Then answer the questions.

An Amazing Race

We were all waiting for the race to begin. There were more than a dozen go-carts. Each one looked the same.

Then Maya and Rafael arrived with their go-cart. People pointed and laughed. Their go-cart looked like a plane! It had wings and a propeller! I was really confused.

Once I went on a plane to Chicago. Anyway, the race started, and of course the plane won. Everyone cheered, and I jumped up and down. Before the plane won, it swooped in the air!

Name _____

1. What is the topic of the story?

_____

_____

2. What details does the speaker give about Maya's go-cart?

_____

_____

3. Which sentence in the recounting is not about the topic?

_____

_____

4. Which sentence in the recounting is out of order?

_____

_____

_____

5. What are two questions you might ask the speaker?

_____

_____

_____

_____

Name _____

Words to Know

Word Bank

almost	become	begin	high	kind
might	night	open	opened	one

▶ Write a word from the box to complete each sentence.

1. It will _____ colder.

2. It might snow at _____ .

3. Then the snow will _____ to fly.

4. We will see it _____ in the hills.

5. I will have _____ hot drink.

6. What _____ will I make?

7. I _____ the milk.

8. It is _____ time to see snow!

Name _____

Long *i* Patterns; Silent Letters

You can spell the /ī/ sound with *igh*, as in *night, i,* as in *sign, y,* as in *spy,* or *i*-consonant-*e,* as in *write.*

Some words have silent letters, such as the *g* in *sign.*

▶ Write each basic Spelling Word in the correct box.

Words with *igh*

_____

_____

_____

_____

Words with *i*

_____

_____

_____

_____

Words with *i* (VCe)

_____

_____

Words with *y*

_____

_____

Spelling Words

Basic

night

kind

spy

child

knife

find

right

high

write

climb

sign

sigh

Review

both

own

roast

float

Name _____

Long *i* Patterns

The long *i* sound has different spellings. The word *bike* has the VC*e* pattern for long *i*. The words *tie* and *sigh* have long *i* vowel teams, *ie*, *igh*. The letter *i* can spell long *i* in open syllables, as in *pilot*, and in words that break the closed syllable rule, as in *kind*. The letter *y* can spell long *i* at the end of a word or syllable, as in *myself*.

▶ Choose and write the word that completes each sentence.

1. We need a new _____bulb for the lamp.

   lie   **line**   **light**

2. I can help you _____ the knot.

   tightly   **untie**   **retile**

3. The lost _____ began to cry.

   child   **chime**   **chimp**

4. Hang the wet pants on the line to _____ .

   die   **dry**   **drive**

5. Getting a prize can _____ your day!

   brick   **bringing**   **brighten**

Name _____

Long *i* Patterns; Silent Letters

You can spell /ī/ with *igh,* as in *right, i,* as in *child, y,* as in *spy,* or *i*-consonant-*e,* as in *knife.*

Some words have silent letters, such as the *k* in *knife.*

▶ Read each clue. Unscramble the word. Write the Spelling Word correctly on the line.

1. A little boy or girl   **dlhic**   _____

2. Breathe out slowly   **ishg**   _____

3. Not left   **trhgi**   _____

4. Used to cut things   **fenik**   _____

5. Not low   **hhig**   _____

6. Not day   **tinhg**   _____

7. Do to a lost thing   **fdni**   _____

8. Really nice   **dink**   _____

▶ Choose other Spelling Words. Scramble them. Ask a partner to write them correctly.

Spelling Words
Basic
night
kind
spy
child
knife
find
right
high
write
climb
sign
sigh
Review
both
own
roast
float

Name _____

Power Words: Yes or No?

Word Bank

honored	success	rare	relay

▶ Read each sentence. Circle **YES** if the word makes sense or **NO** if it does not. Rewrite the sentence so it makes sense.

1. Baseball is a **rare** sport in America.

    YES   NO

    _____

    _____

2. Runners on a **relay** team must run fast for the team to have **success**.

    YES   NO

    _____

3. A famous person may be **honored** with a statue.

    YES   NO

    _____

Name _____

Text Features

Authors may use different text features to organize information. This makes the information easier for the reader to find. **Captions** are words or sentences about photos. **Headings** are titles for a page or section of text. **Fact boxes** give extra information about a topic.

▶ Answer the questions about *Wilma Rudolph: Against All Odds*.

🔍 Pages 108–110 What information do the headings give you? Do you think "Little Wilma" is a good heading for page 108? Explain.

_____

_____

_____

_____

🔍 Pages 112–113 What do you learn from these captions? What information do you learn in the fact box? Why didn't the author put this information in the main text?

_____

_____

_____

_____

_____

Phonics Review

There are many spellings for long *i*. The word *mile* has the VC*e* pattern for long *i*. The words *lie* and *high* have long *i* vowel teams, *ie*, *igh*. The letter *i* can spell long *i* in open syllables, an in *silent*, and in words that break the closed syllable rule, as in *wild*. The letter *y* can spell long *i* at the end of a word or syllable, as in *dry*.

▶ Choose and write the word that completes each sentence.

1. I _____ to make Dad a pie.

    describe   decide   define

2. First, I get all the _____ I need.

    spines   spices   spies

3. Then, I _____ everything in a bowl.

    comb   comment   combine

4. I roll out the _____ crust to put on top.

    magpie   necktie   pie

5. But I cannot use the stove by _____ .

    nearby   myself   shyest

6. To my _____ , Dad comes home just in time.

    delight   slight   design

Name _____

Prefix dis–

The **prefix** *dis–* means "not" or "opposite." You can use the meaning of the prefix and the **base word** to figure out the meaning of a new word. When you are not sure about the meaning of a base word, you can use a dictionary.

Word Bank

disappear   disbelieve   disconnect

► Complete each sentence using a word from the box. If you are unsure about the meaning of a word, you can look it up in the dictionary.

1. If you _____ the telephone, you will not receive the call.

2. It is easy to _____ that you flew to the moon last night!

3. Jasmine likes to watch the deer _____ into the woods.

► Add the word part *dis–* to each word. Then write a sentence using the new word. If you are not sure of the base word's meaning, check a dictionary.

4. please: _____

5. place: _____

Name _____

Power Words: Draw and Write

Word Bank

advice   earned   equal   politics

▶ Draw a picture or write words that will help you remember each Power Word from *Great Leaders.* Try to write more than you draw.

1. advice

2. earned

3. equal

4. politics

Name _____

Ideas and Support

When authors write to **persuade**, they want readers to agree with them or to do something. First, an author states an **opinion** that tells what they think or believe. Then they give **reasons** to support the opinion. Strong reasons include **facts**, or things that can be proved. That helps persuade the reader to agree with the author.

▶ Answer the questions about *Great Leaders*.

🔍 Pages 122–125 What does Olivia think of Abigail Adams? Is this a fact or an opinion? Explain. How do the examples about what Abigail did for women's rights help Olivia persuade readers?

_____

_____

_____

_____

_____

🔍 Pages 126–130 What belief does Anthony share with readers? Is this a fact or an opinion? What does Anthony want readers to do?

_____

_____

_____

_____

Name _____

Words to Know

▶ Write the word that best completes each sentence.

1. Max will _____ a tale.

2. He will make a _____ .

3. June will help with the _____ book.

4. It will be _____ book.

5. It will take them two _____ to write.

6. Max _____ of the tale.

7. Max and June are _____ to write.

8. The two _____ them will have fun!

Word Bank

began

book

of

ready

their

thought

two

whole

write

years

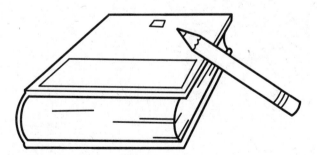

Name _____

Homophones

Homophones are words that sound the same but have different spellings and meanings. *Be* and *bee* are homophones.

▶ Write the basic Spelling Words as homophone pairs.

Homophone Pairs

_____   _____

_____   _____

_____   _____

_____   _____

_____   _____

Spelling Words
Basic
meet
meat
week
weak
mane
main
tail
tale
be
bee
too
two
Review
child
night
high
spy

Name _____

Suffixes –ful, –less

A suffix is a syllable, or word part, added to the end of a word to change its meaning. The suffix –less means "without," as in *spotless*. The suffix –ful means "full of," as in *skillful*.

▶ Write the word that describes the picture.

Is it **painful** or **painless**?	Is it **useful** or **useless**?

_____	_____
Is this **hopeful** or **hopeless**?	Is she **graceful** or **graceless**?
_____	_____
Is it **restful** or **restless**?	Is it **helpful** or **helpless**?

_____	_____

Name _____

Homophones

Homophones are words that sound the same but have different spellings and meanings. *Tail* and *tale* are homophones.

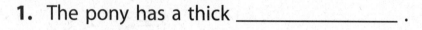

▶ Write the Spelling Word that best completes each sentence.

1. The pony has a thick _____ .

2. The _____ is in its hive.

3. Our teacher told us a tall _____ .

4. _____ me at the bus stop.

5. Joe and Jay are my _____ brothers.

6. A dog wags its _____ .

7. When will you _____ home?

8. Let us drive on the _____ road.

9. Is there _____ in your sandwich?

10. Are you going to the game, _____ ?

▶ Write two more sentences with missing Spelling Words, like the ones on this page. Trade with a partner. Complete each other's sentences.

Spelling Words
Basic
meet
meat
week
weak
mane
main
tail
tale
be
bee
too
two
Review
child
night
high
spy

Name _____

Power Words: Match

Word Bank

capital	charge	council	laws
members	state	solve	troop

▶ Write the Power Word from *Who Are Government's Leaders?* that best fits each item.

1. Which word names a place with many towns and cities? _____

2. This is a word that names a group of people in a club. _____

3. These are rules that keep people safe. _____

4. Which word names the action of someone who leads a group? _____

5. Which word names a group of people who are leaders? _____

6. This is where leaders of a government meet. _____

7. These are people who belong to a group. _____

8. A clue will help a detective do this to a problem. _____

Content-Area Words

Some informational texts have special words about a social studies or science topic. Readers may use **context clues** to figure out the meaning of these **content-area words**. Context clues are the words and sentences around an unfamiliar word that can be clues to its meaning.

▶ Answer the questions about *Who Are Government's Leaders?*

🔍 Page 138 Which sentence on this page helps you define *governor*? Why was this sentence more helpful than the one before it? How else could you find the meaning of this word?

_____

_____

_____

_____

_____

🔍 Page 139 Does what you know about the word *citizens* fit the way the word is used here? Explain.

_____

_____

_____

Name _____

Phonics Review

- A suffix is a syllable, or word part, added to the end of a word to change its meaning. The words *useful* and *useless* have suffixes. The suffix –*ful* means "full of." The suffix –*less* means "without."

- When a two-syllable word ends with a consonant followed by –*y*, change the *y* to *i* before adding the suffix: *penny*, *penniless*.

▶ Read the sentences. Add a suffix to the base word in dark print to complete the sentences.

–ful	–less

1. There is no **wind**.

   A kite will not fly on a _____ day.

2. Recess is a time to run and **play**.

   That is when the kids are _____ .

3. Do not **waste** your lunch.

   It is _____ to toss it away.

4. I made **plenty** of snacks for the picnic.

   The snacks will be _____ .

5. Most birds have wings they use in **flight**.

   But an ostrich is a _____ bird.

Name _____

Words That Name People

Nouns are words that name people, places, or things. Nouns that name people tell who they are, what they do, or give a title. If you do not know what a noun means, you can look it up in a dictionary.

▶ Draw a picture for each noun. If you are unsure about the noun, you can look it up in a dictionary.

1. baker	2. firefighter

Word Bank

baby	grandfather	pilot	queen

▶ Write the noun from the box that best completes each sentence. If you are not sure of a word's meaning, check the dictionary.

3. I visit my _____ every Sunday.

4. The _____ is the leader of her country.

5. The _____ will fly the airplane.

6. The cute _____ crawled toward the toy.

Name _____

Words to Know

Knowing how to read and write these words can make you a better reader and writer.

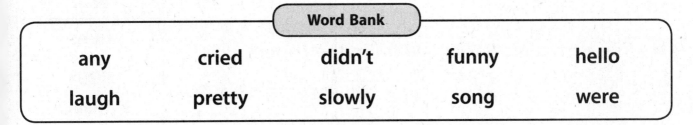

Word Bank				
any	cried	didn't	funny	hello
laugh	pretty	slowly	song	were

▶ Write a word from the box to complete each sentence.

1. Rick waved _____ .

2. Beth and I _____ glad to see him.

3. Rick sang a _____ .

4. He sang it _____ .

5. It is a _____ song.

6. It got so pretty that I _____ !

7. Beth told a funny joke to make me _____ .

8. She _____ want to see me cry.

9. Can we hear _____ fun songs?

Name _____

Inflections -s, -es

To spell the plural of most words, add –s, as in *egg<u>s</u>*.
To spell the plural of words ending in *s, x,* and *sh,*
add –es, as in *box<u>es</u>*.

▶ Write each basic Spelling Word in the correct
column.

Plurals with –s	Plurals with –es
_____	_____
_____	_____
_____	_____
_____	_____
_____	_____
_____	_____
_____	_____

Spelling Words

Basic

hens

eggs

ducks

bikes

boxes

wishes

dresses

names

bells

stamps

dishes

grapes

Review

too

two

tail

tale

Name _____

Suffixes –y, –ly

A suffix is a syllable, or word part, added to the end of a word to change its meaning. The suffix –y means "like" or "full of." The suffix –ly means "in that way."

▶ Complete each sentence. Use each word from the box once.

windy	chilly	wildly	lovely	hilly
quickly	rainy	snowy	sunny	

1. I can look out my window to _____ plan my day.

2. On a _____ day, I can fly a _____ kite.

3. On a _____ day, I can stomp _____ in the mud.

4. On a _____ day, I can ride my sled down

   a _____ slope.

5. On a hot, _____ day, I can escape the heat

   in a _____ lake.

Name _____

Inflections -s, -es

To spell the plural of most words, add –s, as in bell<u>s</u>.
To spell the plural of words ending in s, x, and sh,
add –es, as in dress<u>es</u>

▶ Write –s or –es to make each word plural.
Then write the Spelling Word on the line.

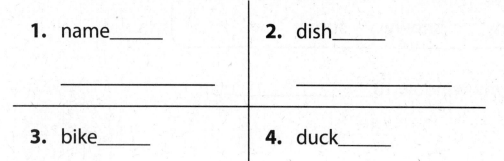

Spelling Words

Basic

hens

eggs

ducks

bikes

boxes

wishes

dresses

names

bells

stamps

dishes

grapes

Review

too

two

tail

tale

1. name_____

   _____

2. dish_____

   _____

3. bike_____

   _____

4. duck_____

   _____

5. dress_____

   _____

6. box_____

   _____

7. stamp_____

   _____

8. egg_____

   _____

9. wish_____

   _____

10. hen_____

    _____

11. grape_____

    _____

12. bell_____

    _____

Name _____

Phonics Review

A suffix is a syllable added to the end of a word to change its meaning. The suffix –y adds the meaning "like." The suffix –ly adds the meaning "in that way." Sometimes, you need to change a spelling before you add a suffix.

- If a word ends in one vowel and one consonant, double the final consonant and add –y. *(fun, funny)*
- If a word ends in final silent *e*, drop the *e* and add –y. *(wave, wavy)*
- If a two-syllable word ends in *y*, change *y* to *i* and add –ly. *(ready, readily)*

▶ Add the suffix to write a new word. Use the spelling rules to help you.

happy + –ly _____	**safe + –ly** _____
mist + –y _____	**fog + –y** _____
wave + –y _____	**handy + –ly** _____

Power Words: Match

<table>
<tr><td colspan="4" align="center">**Word Bank**</td></tr>
<tr><td>clings</td><td>damage</td><td>excess</td><td>funnel</td></tr>
<tr><td>occur</td><td>pellets</td><td>predict</td><td>tough</td></tr>
</table>

▶ Write the Power Word from *Wild Weather* that best fits each item.

1. Which word means the opposite of *easy*?

   _____

2. This word means I have too much of something.

   _____

3. Which word names tiny balls of something?

   _____

4. If you do this, you say what you think will happen in the future.

   _____

5. Which word means the opposite of *fix*?

   _____

6. Which word means *to take place*?

   _____

7. Which word could be a cloud's shape?

   _____

8. This word means the same as *sticks to*.

   _____

Name _____

Suffixes -er, -est

Add –er to the end of an **adjective**, or describing word, to compare two things. Add –est to compare three or more things.

▶ Read the word and look at the pictures. Add –er or –est to the end of the base word. Then write a sentence about the pictures using the new word.

1.

big: _____ : _____

_____

2.

heavy: _____ : _____

_____

▶ Add –er and –est to the base word *easy*. On the lines below, write a sentence using each of the new words.

3. _____ : _____

_____

4. _____ : _____

_____

Name _____

Text Organization

Text organization is the way an author shares information in a text so readers will understand it. Texts organized by **cause** and **effect** describe how one event leads to another event. A cause is something that happens. An effect is what happens because of the cause.

▶ Answer the questions about *Wild Weather*.

🔍 Pages 160–161 What do you notice about the way the author organizes the text on these pages? What causes warm air to rise? What is the effect?

_____

_____

_____

_____

🔍 Pages 168–169 What type of wild weather is Sonny asking about? What does Chuck say is the cause of snowflakes forming? What is the effect of the ground being cold? Why do you think the author organizes the text this way?

_____

_____

_____

_____

Name _____

Homophones

Homophones sound alike but do not have the same spelling or meanings. Look for **context clues** and the word's spelling to figure out its meaning. You can also use a dictionary.

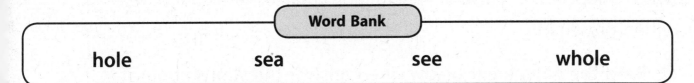

Word Bank
hole   sea   see   whole

▶ Choose a homophone to complete each sentence. Write its meaning on the line.

1. The squirrel dug a _____ to hide a nut.

_____

2. Dad wears glasses to help him _____ what he is reading.

_____

3. Jackson likes to sit on the beach and look at the _____ .

_____

4. Our _____ class will sing a song together at the assembly.

_____

▶ Find each word in a dictionary. Then write a sentence.

5. break: _____

6. brake: _____

Name _____

Digital Tools and Texts

A **digital tool** is a type of technology, like a computer, tablet, or smartphone. A **digital text** is a text you read or experience using digital tools. A **presentation** is a formal way to share information with others. You can use a presentation tool, like a digital slide, when presenting.

▶ Read the digital text below. Then answer questions about it.

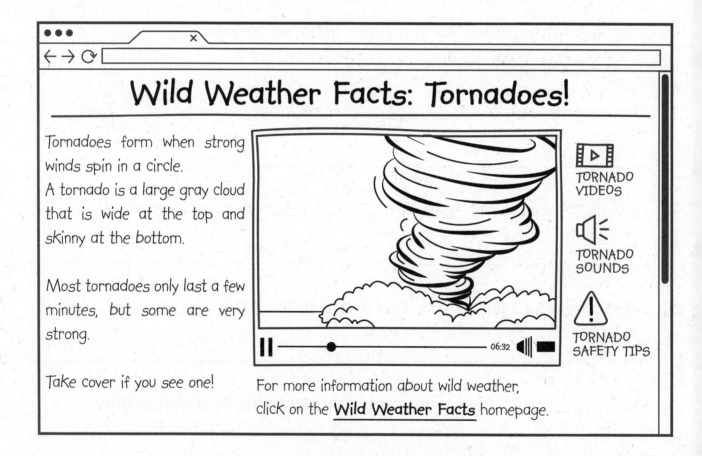

1. What is a digital tool that you could use to find and read this digital text?

_____

2. Circle the letters of the special features you see in "Wild Weather
Facts: Tornadoes!"

   a. Video recording

   b. Hyperlink

   c. Interactive diagram

   d. Audio recording

3. Which special feature would you click on to find information about
other kinds of wild weather?

_____

_____

_____

▶ Share a fact you learned about tornadoes. Write and draw in the box to
make a slide you could use to present the information.

Name _____

Words to Know

▶ Write the word that best completes each sentence.

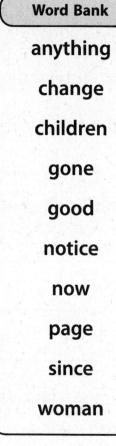

Word Bank

anything

change

children

gone

good

notice

now

page

since

woman

1. It is time for a puppet show _____ .

2. I have not seen a puppet show _____ I moved.

3. The _____ sit down.

4. They _____ nine puppets.

5. A _____ has the puppets.

6. She can _____ their costumes.

7. She reads a _____ in a book to begin.

8. Now the children have _____ home.

9. The children had a _____ time.

10. I like _____ that has puppets in it!

Name _____

Sounds for c and g

Words with *c* may have the /k/ sound, as in *cot*, or the /s/ sound, as in *face*. Words with *g* may have the /g/ sound, as in *goal*, or the /j/ sound, as in *gym*.

▶ Write each basic Spelling Word in the correct box.

Words with /k/

_____

_____

_____

Words with /s/

_____

_____

_____

Words with /g/

_____

_____

_____

Words with /j/

_____

_____

_____

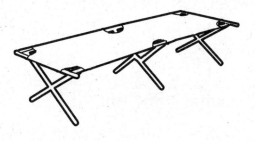

Spelling Words
Basic
cot
face
goal
gym
nice
page
plug
crash
gone
brag
city
trace
Review
stamps
dishes
bells
dresses

Name _____

Prefix dis-

A prefix is a syllable, or word part, added to the beginning of a word to change its meaning. The prefix *dis–* adds the meaning "not" or "the opposite." The word *dislike* has the prefix *dis–*.

▶ Read the sentences. Add the prefix *dis–* to the base word in dark print to complete the sentences.

1. Miss Sands **trusts** the old horse with kids.

   She _____ the young wild horse.

2. A good rest can put your body at **ease**.

   If you have a _____ , you are sick.

3. Ben had something **lodged** in his throat.

   Dad gave him a pat on the back and _____ it.

4. The girls and boys **band** together to play a game.

   They will _____ when the game is over.

5. Mom is **pleased** when we pick up our things.

   She is _____ when we make a mess.

6. I **close** up the gift for Gram in a box.

   I will not _____ what I got her.

Name _____

Sounds for c and g

Words with *c* may have the /k/ sound, as in *crash*, or the /s/ sound, as in *nice*. Words with *g* may have the /g/ sound, as in *plug*, or the /j/ sound, as in *page*.

▶ Write the Spelling Word that best completes each sentence.

1. We play games in the _____ .

2. Paul lives in a big _____ .

3. Read the next _____ of the book.

4. The cat has a black spot on her _____ .

5. At camp, I slept on a _____ .

6. Did you kick a _____ ?

7. Be _____ to your pals.

8. The vase fell with a _____ .

▶ Write four more sentences with missing Spelling Words, like the ones on this page. Trade with a partner. Complete each other's sentences.

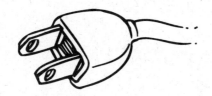

Spelling Words
Basic
cot
face
goal
gym
nice
page
plug
crash
gone
brag
city
trace
Review
stamps
dishes
bells
dresses

Name _____

Power Words: Draw and Write

advantages	average	front	impressed

▶ Draw a picture or write words that will help you remember each Power Word from *Cloudette*. Try to write more than you draw.

1. advantages

2. average

3. front

4. impressed

Name _____

Point of View

Point of view describes the way readers see things happen in a story. If a story is told from first-person point of view, a character in the story is the narrator. A story told from third-person point of view has an outside narrator.

▶ Answer the questions about *Cloudette*.

🔍 Pages 182–183 Is this story written in first-person or third-person point of view? How do you know?

_____

_____

_____

_____

🔍 Pages 186–187 What does the narrator tell about Cloudette? How would the words change if the story were told in first-person point of view?

_____

_____

_____

_____

Name _____

Phonics Review

- The prefix *dis–* adds the meaning "not" or "opposite of" to a base word: *disown*.

- If a word has a long vowel CV*e* pattern, drop the final *e* and then add *–ed* or *–ing*: *trace, traced, tracing*.

- If a word has a short vowel CVC pattern, double the final consonant and then add *–ed* or *–ing*: *tag, tagged, tagging*.

- If a word ends in *y*, change the *y* to *i* before *–ed*, but not for *–ing*: *try, tried, trying*.

▶ Write the word that names the action in the picture.

Add **–ed** to **displease**. _____		Add **–ing** to **sled**. _____	
Add **–ed** to **fry**. _____		Add **–ing** to **dislike**. _____	
Add **–ing** to **cry**. _____		Add **–ing** to **hike**. _____	

Name _____

Prefixes un-, re-

The **prefix** *un–* means "to reverse" or "not." The prefix *re–* means "again." Use the meaning of the prefix and the **base word** to figure out the meaning of the new word. If you are not sure about the meaning of a base word, you can use a dictionary.

▶ Add *un–* or *re–* to each base word below to make a new word. Then draw a line to match the word to its definition.

1. _____happy   not healthy

2. _____healthy   to appear again

3. _____appear   to pay again

4. _____pay   not happy

▶ Circle the word that completes the sentence. Check a dictionary if you are unsure about the meaning of a word.

5. I was bored during the movie because the story was _____ .

   interesting   uninteresting

6. I will _____ the beans, even though I did not like them
   the first time.

   retry   try

7. A story that is fiction is usually _____ .

   untrue   true

Name _____

Power Words: Yes or No?

Word Bank

| flash | gusts | layer | supplies |

▶ Read each sentence. Circle **YES** if the word makes sense or **NO** if it does not. Rewrite the sentence so it makes sense.

1. An extra **layer** of clothing will keep you warm.

YES   NO

_____

2. Bottles of water are good **supplies** to have during a storm.

YES   NO

_____

3. A **flash** of light is not bright.

YES   NO

_____

4. You are more likely to feel **gusts** indoors.

YES   NO

_____

Name _____

Text Features

Authors of informational texts often use different kinds of text features to explain ideas or to help readers find information. A **caption** is words or sentences that describe a picture. A **heading** is the title of a page or section of a text. A **fact box** is a feature with extra information about the topic.

▶ Answer the questions about *Get Ready for Weather*.

🔍 Page 207 How does the caption tell more about the picture? What do the different symbols in the chart stand for?

It tells us waht a medoraligists. it tells us waht the wether will be,

_____

_____

🔍 Pages 208–209 What does the heading tell you about the information you will read in this part of the text? Why did the author put some information about lightning in the Try This! box?

It tells me more abot the page, To give you more infor machon,

_____

_____

Name _____

Words to Know

Word Bank

body	color	dark	hard	hour
large	part	started	warm	was

▶ Circle the word that best completes each sentence.

1. Tess will run in a (large, started) race.

2. It will be (hour, hard).

3. It will take at least one (hour, color).

4. Tess will (warm, part) up.

5. She will move her (body, dark).

6. Then the race will get (warm, started).

7. (Warm, Was) that fun, Tess?

8. Tess says the last (part, dark) was the best.

Name _____

r-Controlled Vowel *ar*

You can spell the /är/ sound with *ar*, as in *car*.

▶ Write each basic Spelling Word in the correct box.

Basic

car	
dark	
card	
star	
park	
yard	
party	
hard	
smart	
start	
part	
spark	

Words ending with *ar*

_____

_____

_____

Words ending with *ark*

_____

_____

_____

Words ending with *ard*

_____

_____

_____

Words ending with *art*

_____

_____

_____

Other words with *ar*

_____

_____

_____

Review

city

crash

goal

gym

r-Controlled Vowel ar

The letters *ar* stand for the *r*-controlled vowel sound you hear in the words *car* and *star*.

▶ Write the word that names the picture. Circle the letters that stand for the *r*-controlled vowel sound you hear in *car*.

card   cart   cars

_____

stark   start   stars

_____

barn   bark   brain

_____

doll   dollar   dolphin

_____

cargo   carpet   carton

_____

grading   garden   garnish

_____

Name _____

r-Controlled Vowel ar

You can spell the /är/ sound with *ar,* as in *star.*

▶ Read each clue. Unscramble the word. Write the Spelling Word correctly on the line.

1. Not light	**kdra**	_____
2. Not soft	**hrad**	_____
3. Land around a home	**dary**	_____
4. Tiny light in the night sky	**rast**	_____
5. Can drive it	**acr**	_____
6. Starts a flame	**kspra**	_____
7. Same as begin	**ttsar**	_____
8. Not a whole	**tpra**	_____

▶ Choose other Spelling Words. Scramble them. Ask a partner to write them correctly.

Power Words: Match

Word Bank

covers	creep	glide	rumble
shimmering	slather	slithering	splatter

▶ Write the Power Word from *Whatever the Weather* that best fits each item.

1. This is a word that means *goes over*. _____

2. This is the sound of thunder. _____

3. Your teacher might use this word to tell you to use a lot of glue. _____

4. Which word describes how something is shining? _____

5. If you see a snake in the grass, it is moving like this. _____

6. Which word can mean the opposite of *run past*? _____

7. This is how drops of a liquid fall. _____

8. Which word describes a smooth and easy movement? _____

Name _____

Elements of Poetry

Poetry is a special kind of writing. Poems have **rhythm, patterns,** and **stanzas.** Some poems **rhyme** or have repetition. Poems also have **descriptive** and **figurative language** to help readers picture what the poet sees in his or her mind.

▶ Answer the questions about *Whatever the Weather*.

🔍 Pages 220–221 What words or phrases does the poet use to help you imagine what the rain sounds like? How do the spaces between the words help create rhythm?

_____

_____

_____

_____

🔍 Page 224 Why did the poet repeat some of the lines in this poem? How does that repetition help you understand the poem's important ideas?

_____

_____

_____

_____

Name _____

Phonics Review

The letters *ar* stand for the *r*-controlled vowel sound you hear in the words *art* and *dark*. Read longer words one syllable at a time. Use the vowel patterns.

► Choose and write a word in each blank to complete the sentences.

1. Mark wants to grow up to be an _____.

   artwork   artful   artless   artist

2. He paints with bright colors like yellow and _____.

   scarf   scarlet   scalp   scarred

3. Mark says his skill comes _____ from his mom.

   partner   party   partly   parch

4. She helped Mark _____ his skills.

   sharpen   shark   shapely   shadow

5. How? Her nice _____ on his art help him do well.

   remakes   remarks   remains   remade

Name _____

Inflections -ed, -ing

Add –ed to the end of a **verb** to tell about an action in the past.
Add –ing to the end of a verb to tell about an action that is
happening in the present or that may happen in the future.

▶ Add –ed or –ing to the word in parentheses to complete
the sentences. Write the word on the line. Remember,
there may be spelling changes to the verb when you
add the ending.

1. (walk) He _____ to school in
   the rain yesterday.

2. (listen) I will be _____ to the weather
   report tomorrow.

3. (hope) Emma is _____ for a sunny day today.

4. (pile) The snow _____ up on the sidewalk
   yesterday.

5. (happen) Another storm will be _____ this week.

▶ Choose one verb about weather: *rain, sleet, snow, melt, flood.*
Write a sentence using each form of the verb.

6. past: _____

7. present: _____

8. future: _____

Name _____

Words to Know

Learn these words. You will see them in your reading and use
them in your writing.

Word Bank

before	example	form	morning	order
store	story	those	word	work

▶ Circle the word that best completes each sentence.

1. I will tell you a (story, store).

2. One (order, morning), my mom got in her car.

3. She was on her way to (word, work).

4. She went to the (store, example) before work.

5. She asked, "Can I (form, order) a cake?"

6. "I like (those, before) cakes," she said.

7. "May I have one (store, word) on it?" she asked.

▶ What word do you think it is? Finish the story using two
new words from the box.

_____

_____

Name _____

r-Controlled Vowels *or*, *ore*

You can spell the /ôr/ sound with *or*, as in *thorn*, or *ore*, as in *chore*.

▶ Write each basic Spelling Word in the correct column.

Words with *or*	Words with *ore*
_____	_____
_____	_____
_____	_____
_____	_____
_____	_____
_____	_____
_____	_____

Spelling Words
Basic
chore
glory
storm
north
store
thorn
morning
snore
stork
worn
tore
forget
Review
star
start
dark
smart

Name _____

r-Controlled Vowels *or, ore*

An *r*-controlled vowel sound is not short or long. The *r* changes the way a vowel sounds. The letters *or* and *ore* stand for the *r*-controlled vowel sound you hear in the words *corn* and *score*.

▶ Choose and write the word that names the picture.

cord core cork  _____	fork fort farm 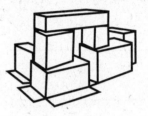 _____
score scorn scorch  _____	seashore seahorse seaport  _____
docket doctor dockyard  _____	accent across acorn  _____

Name _____

r-Controlled Vowels *or, ore*

You can spell the /ôr/ sound with *or*, as in *stork*, or *ore*, as in *store*.

▶ Read each sentence. Cross out the Spelling Word that is spelled incorrectly. Write it correctly on the line.

1. A starm is coming. _____

2. Don't foreget to call me. _____

3. I shop at that stor. _____

4. Ben toor his shirt. _____

5. Have you woren that hat? _____

6. The team hopes for glorey. _____

7. I woke up this murning. _____

8. Did you do the chor yet? _____

9. A storek flew by. _____

▶ Write three sentences with the basic Spelling Words you did not use. Then trade with a partner. Check each other's spelling.

Spelling Words
Basic
chore
glory
storm
north
store
thorn
morning
snore
stork
worn
tore
forget
Review
star
start
dark
smart

Name _____

Phonics Review

The letters *or* and *ore* stand for the *r*-controlled vowel sound you hear in the words *for* and *more*.

Read longer words one syllable at a time. Use the vowel patterns.

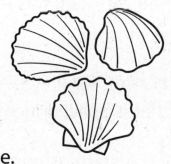

▶ Choose and write a word to complete each sentence.

1. The Morris family went to the _____ one morning.

   season   **seashore**   **seahorse**

2. "Do not _____ sunscreen!" Mrs. Morris called out.

   forget   **former**   **forgive**

3. Morgan wore a cap with a _____ to block the sun.

   visit   **vice**   **visor**

4. He wants to build a sand _____ with a flag on top.

   fort   **fork**   **ford**

5. Cora plans to _____ the beach and pick up shells.

   express   **export**   **explore**

6. Dad will take photos of the boats in the _____ .

   harbor   **foghorn**   **hornet**

Power Words: Match

Word Bank

approached	communicate	deal	figured
motioned	potential	selfless	series

▶ Write the Power Word from *I Am Helen Keller* that best fits each item.

1. When you speak or write a message, you do this.   _____

2. Which word means *came close to*?   _____

3. Several books that have the same characters are part of this.   _____

4. Which word describes how you get along with other people?   _____

5. You act like this when you put a friend's needs before your own.   _____

6. Which word means *came to understand*?   _____

7. You have this because you are working hard toward your future.   _____

8. Which word describes how you asked a friend to come closer?   _____

Name _____

Suffixes –ful, –less

A **suffix** is a word part added to the end of a base word. It changes the base word's meaning. The suffix –ful means "full of." The suffix –less means "without." Use a dictionary to find the meaning of base words that you do not know.

▶ Add the suffix –ful or –less to the word that is in parentheses ( ) to complete each sentence.

1. I am tired because I had a (sleep) _____ night.

2. A (power) _____ storm kept me awake.

3. My little sister was (fear) _____ of the thunder.

4. I told her that thunder was (harm) _____ .

5. Finally, the storm was over and everything became
   (peace) _____ .

▶ Add –ful or –less to each word. Tell what the new word means. If you are unsure about the meaning of the base word, use a dictionary to look up the meaning of the word.

6. end: _____ means _____

7. truth: _____ means _____

Comprehension

Name _____

Text Features

Punctuation marks are **text features** that tell readers when and how long to pause. The dash (—) is a clue to take a short pause. **Ellipses,** or three small dots, mean to pause for a little longer. Words in all capital letters tell you to read that part of the text with more feeling.

▶ Answer the questions about *I Am Helen Keller*.

🔍 Pages 15 and 18 What does the author want you to do when you get to the dots, or ellipses, on page 15? What does the dash tell you to do? Why do you think the author wants you to pause?

_____

_____

_____

_____

🔍 Pages 23–24 What do you notice about the words "YOU UNDERSTAND!!" on page 23? How does the author want you to read these words? Why?

_____

_____

_____

_____

Shades of Meaning

Synonyms are words that mean the same or almost the same thing.
Shades of meaning are the small differences in meaning between synonyms.

Word Bank					
adore	fantastic	full	good	like	stuffed

▶ Write the synonyms from the box that best show shades of meaning.

Least	Greater	Greatest
1. _____	packed	_____
2. _____	love	_____
3. _____	great	_____

Word Bank		
hot	boiling	warm

▶ Choose the best word from the box to complete each sentence.

4. The soup in the pot is _____ on the stove.

5. When the soup is too _____, I wait for it to cool.

6. I like to eat _____ soup on a cold day.

Name _____

Research Questions

When you **research**, you find out information about a topic. Follow these steps to select questions for a research plan.

1. Write questions about your topic.

2. Remove questions that are off topic.

3. Remove questions that can be answered with *yes* or *no*.

4. Group similar questions together.

Research Prompt: Think of someone from history whose life interests you. What questions do you have about his or her life?

1. Write six questions about your topic. Remember to use your senses to help write your questions.

My topic: _____

_____

_____

_____

Name _____

_____

_____

_____

_____

2. Cross out any questions in your list that are not about your topic.

3. Cross out any questions in your list that can be answered with *yes* or *no*.

4. Group questions about similar things together by writing them in the same box in the chart. Add more boxes if you need them.

My Topic:		
Questions about _____	**Questions about** _____	**Questions about** _____

Name _____

Words to Know

▶ Write the word that best completes each sentence.
Not all words will be used.

1. I will take a trip with my _____ .

2. We will leave _____ we pack
   the car.

3. This trip will be _____ than our
   last one.

4. We go _____ hills.

5. Then we stop at the _____ .

6. I will jump in the _____ .

7. I know how to go _____
   the water.

8. We have fun _____ on our trip.

Word Bank
after
better
father
letter
over
paper
river
together
under
water

▶ Write a sentence for a word you did not use yet.

_____

_____

Name _____

r-Controlled Vowel *er*

You can spell the /ûr/ sound with the letters *er*, as in *cracker*.

▶ Write each basic Spelling Word in the correct column.

Words with *er* in the middle	Words with *er* at the end
_____	_____
_____	_____
_____	_____
_____	_____
_____	_____
_____	_____
_____	_____

<table>
<tr><td>Spelling Words</td></tr>
</table>

Basic

father

over

under

herd

water

verb

paper

cracker

offer

cover

germ

master

Review

morning

forget

glory

north

Name _____

r-Controlled Vowels *er, ir, ur*

An *r*-controlled vowel sound is not short or long. The *r* changes the way a vowel sounds. The letters *er*, *ir*, and *ur* stand for the *r*-controlled vowel sound you hear in *girl*.

▶ Write the word that names the picture. Then circle the letters that stand for the vowel sound in *girl*.

trumpet twirling twitches	**thermal threat thermos**

_____	_____
perch parts purse	**sunshine sunburn sunflower**

_____	_____
gingerly gerbils germs	**birdcage blackbird surprise**

_____	_____

Name _____

r-Controlled Vowel *er*

You can spell the /ûr/ sound with the letters *er*, as in *paper*.

▶ Write the Spelling Word that best completes each sentence.

1. How many cows are in the _____ ?

2. The dog is _____ the chair.

3. My _____ coaches my team.

4. He stepped _____ the log.

5. The _____ in the lake is cold.

6. May I _____ you a snack?

7. I ate cheese on a _____ .

8. You can write on the _____ .

▶ Write four more sentences with missing Spelling Words, like the ones on this page. Then trade with a partner. Complete each other's sentences.

192

Spelling Words

Basic

father

over

under

herd

water

verb

paper

cracker

offer

cover

germ

master

Review

morning

forget

glory

north

Name _____

Power Words: Yes or No?

Word Bank			
arrange	current	statements	timeline

► Read each sentence. Circle **YES** if the word makes sense or **NO** if it does not. Rewrite the sentence so it makes sense.

1. You should **arrange** flowers on a plate.

   YES   NO

   _____

2. The **current** year begins with the number 2.

   YES   NO

   _____

3. You may answer questions with **statements**.

   YES   NO

   _____

4. A **timeline** shows events in alphabetical order.

   YES   NO

   _____

Name _____

Text Organization

Informational texts have a type of **text organization** that fits the topic and the author's purpose. Authors use **chronological order** when they describe the order of the steps in a process. Clue words like *first*, *then*, *next*, and *finally*—and text features like numbered steps—help readers follow the steps.

▶ Answer the questions about *How to Make a Timeline*.

🔍 Pages 44–45 What do all of the events on Tramayne's timeline have in common? How did Tramayne organize the events on his timeline? What clues help you know?

_____

_____

_____

_____

🔍 Page 46 How are the timeline directions and materials organized? Why did the author organize them like this?

_____

_____

_____

_____

Name _____

Phonics Review

The letters *er*, *ir*, and *ur* stand for the vowel sound in *girl*. The letters *are*, *air*, and *ear* can stand for the vowel sound in *hair*. Read longer words one syllable at a time.

▶ Choose and write two words to complete each sentence.

1. Claire is taking her _____ ride

   in an _____ .

       thirst   **first**   **airplane**   **armchair**

2. "Do not be _____ !" said her

   _____ Gwen.

       stopper   **shared**   **sister**   **scared**

3. A person _____ a uniform

   _____ snacks.

       staring   **served**   **wearing**   **weaker**

4. Soon the plane _____ and landed at the

   _____ .

       airtime   **turning**   **airport**   **turned**

5. "Let's _____ and find _____ ,"

   said Gwen.

       hurry   **hunger**   **birthday**   **Grandmother**

Name _____

Prefix pre–

The **prefix** *pre–* means "before." Use the meaning of the
prefix and the **base word** to figure out the meaning of
the new word. If you are not sure about the meaning of
a base word, you can look the word up in a dictionary.

▶ Use the words in parentheses ( ) to write a word with the prefix
pre– to complete each sentence.

1. Mom will _____ our clothes before she puts
   (sort before)
   them in the washer.

2. I like to look at the _____ sky.
   (before dawn)

3. Mr. Muñoz will _____ our plan for the project.
   (approve before)

4. The sandwiches in the cafeteria were _____ .
   (made before)

5. If you _____ the oven, it will be warm
   (heat before)
   when we are ready to cook.

6. Nate _____ for the tickets to the game.
   (paid before)

7. Lila settles into her seat _____ .
   (before the flight)

Name _____

Power Words: Draw and Write

Word Bank

ashamed   elders   overflowing   pride

▶ Draw a picture or write words that will help you remember each Power Word from *The Stories He Tells: The Story of Joseph Bruchac.* Try to write more than you draw.

1. ashamed

2. elders

3. overflowing

4. pride

Name _____

Author's Purpose

Authors write to **persuade**, **inform**, or **entertain**. How can you find the author's purpose? First, look for clues about the genre. Then, ask questions about what you read and find answers.

▶ Answer the questions about *The Stories He Tells: The Story of Joseph Bruchac*.

🔍 Pages 52–54 What clues about the genre of this text help you know what type of text you are reading?

_____

_____

_____

_____

🔍 Pages 58–60 What do you think is the author's purpose for writing this text? What makes this author's perspective about Joseph Bruchac special?

_____

_____

_____

_____

Name _____

Words to Know

Word Bank

air	city	friend	hair	heard
learn	looked	stood	street	remember

▶ Read the riddles and sentences below. Write the correct word from the Word Bank.

1. A pal is a _____ . _____

2. It is on your head. _____

3. It is a big place. _____

4. Cars go on this. _____

5. In school, we _____ . _____

6. Don't forget. _____

7. Planes fly in the _____ . _____

8. Last week, I _____ in line for tickets. _____

▶ Write a sentence for a word you did not use yet.

_____

Name _____

Vowel Team oo /o͞o/

You can spell the /o͞o/ sound with the letters *oo*, as in *books*.

▶ Write each basic Spelling Word in the correct box.

Words with
ook

_____

_____

_____

_____

_____

Words with
ood

_____

_____

_____

_____

_____

Words with
oof

_____

_____

Words with
oot

_____

_____

Name _____

Vowel Team oo

The vowel team *oo* has two sounds. You can hear the different sounds in the words *cook* and *moose*.

► Read the words. Three words name things that are alike in some way. Write the word that does not belong.

1. moo   coo

   cook   hoot   _____

2. noon   hoof

   foot   tooth   _____

3. coop   igloo

   notebook   bedroom   _____

4. goose   caboose

   raccoon   rooster   _____

5. sooner   groomer

   roofer   zookeeper   _____

6. cooler   unhook

   toolbox   bookcase   _____

Name _____

Vowel Team oo /ŏŏ/

You can spell the /ŏŏ/ sound with the letters *oo*, as in *foot*.

▶ Read each clue. Unscramble the word. Write the Spelling Word correctly on the line.

1. You can read them.   **ksobo** _____

2. Do this on a stove.   **okco** _____

3. A horse's foot   **fooh** _____

4. A small corner   **ookn** _____

5. Part of a jacket   **ohod** _____

6. Opposite of *sat*   **doost** _____

7. It comes from trees.   **dowo** _____

8. Opposite of *gave*   **ootk** _____

9. Part of your body   **ofto** _____

▶ Choose other Spelling Words. Make up a clue for each one. Scramble the letters. Ask a partner to write the words correctly.

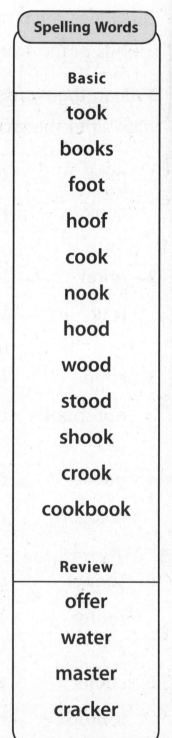

Spelling Words
Basic
took
books
foot
hoof
cook
nook
hood
wood
stood
shook
crook
cookbook
Review
offer
water
master
cracker

Name _____

Power Words: Match

Word Bank

allowed	alone	dared	deserved
reminding	secret	starlit	whir

▶ Write the Power Word from *Drum Dream Girl* that best fits each item.

1. Which word describes a nighttime sky? _____

2. This describes you when you are all by yourself. _____

3. You may whisper this into your friend's ear. _____

4. When someone tells you again, they are doing this. _____

5. Which word means *was brave enough to do something*? _____

6. A fan and a car's engine may all make this noise. _____

7. Which word means the opposite of *had not earned*? _____

8. If someone says something is okay to do, it is this. _____

Name _____

Setting

The **setting** of a story is where and when a story or poem takes place. Authors give **details**, or small bits of information, to **describe** the setting. Readers can ask, "Why is the setting important to the story?" to understand what is happening in the story and why.

▶ Answer the questions about *Drum Dream Girl.*

🔍 Pages 66–71 Where does the drum dream girl live? What clues in the illustrations tell you more about her home?

_____

_____

_____

_____

🔍 Pages 72–78 Where does the girl go? Why are these different places important to the poem?

_____

_____

_____

_____

Name _____

Phonics Review

The vowel team *oo* has two sounds. You can hear the different sounds in the words *cook* and *moose*.

Read longer words one syllable at a time. Use the vowel patterns.

▶ Choose and write the word that answers the clue.

1. This is a time of the day.   _____

      moonbeam   **afternoon**   **goose**

2. You are this when you act silly.   _____

      goody   **goofy**   **gloomy**

3. You see this in the night sky.   _____

      moonwalk   **moonlight**   **moonstruck**

4. A person does this in a kitchen.   _____

      cooking   **uncooked**   **cookout**

5. This means the opposite of *later*.   _____

      roofer   **sooner**   **looser**

6. This plant may grow in the woods.   _____

      bedroom   **raccoon**   **mushroom**

Name _____

Compound Words

Compound words are made up of two smaller words. Knowing the smaller words can help you read, spell, and know the meaning of the compound word. Use a dictionary to check if your meaning is correct.

▶ Draw a line to divide each compound word into two smaller words. Then write the meaning of the compound word. Use a dictionary to check if your meaning is correct.

1. sunrise _____

2. backpack _____

3. raincoat _____

4. lunchroom _____

5. mailbox _____

▶ Read the word pairs and write the compound word on the line.

6. base, ball _____

7. hall, way _____

8. sea, horse _____

Name _____

Words to Know

Knowing how to read and write these words can make you a better reader and writer.

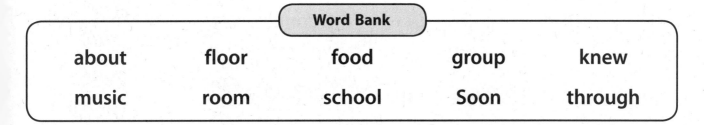

Word Bank

about	floor	food	group	knew
music	room	school	Soon	through

▶ Fill in the blanks with words from the box to complete the sentences.

1. Jay has fun at _____ .

2. He likes to go to the art _____ .

3. Jay walks _____ the hall.

4. Then he walks to the _____ room.

5. He sits on the _____ and sings.

6. _____ he sees Mark.

7. Mark and Jay see another _____ of kids.

8. Jay and Mark eat _____ with the kids.

Vowel Patterns: /o͞o/

You can spell the /o͞o/ sound with *oo*, as in *spoon*, *ew*, as in *crew*, or *ou*, as in *you*.

▶ Write each basic Spelling Word in the correct column.

Words with *oo*	Words with *ew*	Words with *ou*
_____	_____	_____
_____	_____	_____
_____	_____	_____
_____	_____	_____
_____	_____	_____

Spelling Words

Basic

root

crew

spoon

bloom

grew

room

you

stew

boost

scoop

flew

threw

Review

crook

shook

stood

cookbook

Name _____

Vowel Patterns: /o͞o/

The vowel patterns *o, oo, ew, ou,* and *ue* can all stand for the same vowel sound you hear in *moose.*

▶ Read the question and look at the picture. Write the word that answers the question.

Can it **scoop** or **stew**?

_____

Is it a **group** or a **groom**?

_____

Is it **wooden** or **woolen**?

_____

Is it a **blueprint** or a **bluebird**?

_____

Is it a **toadstool** or **stepstool**?

_____

Is it a **bookmark** or **notebook**?

_____

Name _____

Vowel Patterns: /o͞o/

You can spell the /o͞o/ sound with *oo*, as in *root*, *ew*, as in *stew*, or *ou*, as in *you*.

▶ Write the missing letter or letters. Then write the Spelling Word on the line.

1. st_____   _____

2. r_____t   _____

3. b_____st   _____

4. sp_____n   _____

5. cr_____   _____

6. bl_____m   _____

7. thr_____   _____

8. gr_____   _____

9. sc_____p   _____

10. fl_____   _____

▶ Write two sentences with the basic Spelling Words you did not use. Then trade with a partner. Check each other's spelling.

Spelling Words
Basic
root
crew
spoon
bloom
grew
room
you
stew
boost
scoop
flew
threw
Review
crook
shook
stood
cookbook

Phonics Review

The vowel team *oo* can stand for the vowel sounds you hear in *cook* and *moose*. The vowel patterns *o*, *ew*, *ou*, and *ue* can all stand for the same vowel sound you hear in *moose*.

Read longer words one syllable at a time. Use the vowel patterns.

▶ Choose and write two words to complete each sentence.

1. Lewis needs _____ to make a wooden

   _____ .

   foolish   **spoonful**   **plywood**   **footstool**

2. Lou and his brother _____ _____ .

   today   **argued**   **approve**   **afternoon**

3. Birds like _____ fly _____ the
   rain forest.

   into   **toucans**   **tissues**   **unglued**

4. Sue will _____ her dance _____ .

   issue   **remove**   **routine**   **improve**

5. The horses like _____ _____ carrots.

   chewing   **grouping**   **uncooked**   **clueless**

Power Words: Match

| fuels | minerals | moisten | process |
| provides | seedlings | spiky | sprout |

▶ Write the Power Word from *Experiment with What a Plant Needs to Grow* that best fits each item.

1. To do this to a sponge, I would dip it into a pail of water. _____

2. Which word describes something that is sharp and pointy? _____

3. What do all plants and animals need to grow? _____

4. These are young plants. _____

5. Which word describes the action of giving a thing power? _____

6. You follow steps in order to complete this. _____

7. This is the action of a new plant breaking through the soil. _____

8. Which word means the opposite of *takes away*? _____

Name _____

Inflections -s, -es

The endings –s and –es added to the end of a **singular noun**
makes it **plural**, or changes the number of something. The
ending –s or –es added to the end of a **verb** shows that an
action is happening now, or in the present.

▶ Add –s or –es to the word in bold. If the word you changed
is a noun, circle *Noun*. If the word you changed is a verb,
circle *Verb*.

1. The hungry bird **search** _____ for a worm   Noun   Verb
   to eat.

2. Do you know why some **animal** _____   Noun   Verb
   sleep so much?

3. The cook **mix** _____ together eggs,   Noun   Verb
   flour, and milk.

4. He turned on all the light **switch** _____   Noun   Verb
   in the house.

5. Martin washed two **cup** _____ in the sink.   Noun   Verb

6. The dentist gave us new **toothbrush** _____ .   Noun   Verb

7. Didi **play** _____ with her friends every   Noun   Verb
   Saturday.

8. Nana **get** _____ her mail at the same   Noun   Verb
   time every day.

Name _____

Text Organization

Text organization is the way an author shares information so readers will understand it. Authors organize texts to fit the topic and their purpose for writing. One way to organize text is by **cause** and **effect**. A cause is why something happens, and an effect is what happens as a result of a cause.

▶ Answer the questions about *Experiment with What a Plant Needs to Grow.*

🔍 Pages 105–108 What caused the seeds in the cotton balls to not grow well? What was the effect of giving the seeds no water? What do you notice about how the text is organized?

_____

_____

_____

_____

🔍 Page 111 What is the cause of the leaves starting to wilt? What is the effect of putting petroleum jelly on the bottom of the leaves? Why do you think the author organizes the text around causes and effects?

_____

_____

_____

_____

Reference Sources

When you are reading, you may see a word you do not know.
Use a **dictionary** or a **glossary** to find out the word's meaning,
how to say it, and how to spell it. Words in a dictionary or a
glossary are listed in **alphabetical order**.

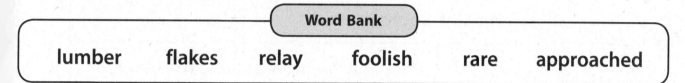

Word Bank

lumber   flakes   relay   foolish   rare   approached

▶ Write the words from the box in alphabetical order.

1. _____   4. _____

2. _____   5. _____

3. _____   6. _____

▶ Look up these words in a glossary or dictionary: *frigid, beamed*.
Write the words next to the picture that shows the word's meaning.
Check that you spelled each word correctly.

7.
   _____

8.
   _____

Name _____

Choose and Use Sources

Before writing a book, authors have to research information about their topic. Research sources include **experts**, **primary sources**, and **secondary sources**. Sources can also be print or digital. Print sources include books, pictures, and magazines. Websites and videos are digital sources.

Types of Sources	
Experts	People who know information about a topic because of their job or education
Primary Sources	Original documents, such as diaries, interviews, or research results
Secondary Sources	Books, reports, or articles that someone wrote using primary sources

1. Would a letter written by Abraham Lincoln be a primary or secondary source? _____

2. A person writes a new book about pine trees using the research results someone else wrote. Is the new book a primary or secondary source? _____

Name _____

Put a checkmark next to sources you would use to answer the research question below. If it's a source you would use, write if it is an expert, primary, or secondary source.

Research question: How do plants use sunlight to make food?

1. Research by a scientist who studies plants

☐ Type of source: _____

2. A book about how to stay safe in the sun

☐ Type of source: _____

3. A person who teaches others about plants

☐ Type of source: _____

4. A website about plants that someone made using primary sources

☐ Type of source: _____

Authors list the sources they use when researching a topic. Find two sources with information about plants. Then write your sources on the lines below.

1. Name of author _____

   Title of source _____

2. Name of author _____

   Title of source _____

Name _____

Words to Know

▶ Write the word that best completes each sentence. Not all words will be used.

1. The boys will paint a _____ .

2. It is a big house in _____ .

3. The boys _____ a paint can on the porch.

4. The house will be _____ .

5. It is thick _____ paint.

6. Do you hear that _____ ?

7. Let's _____ to the boys sing as they paint!

8. One has a low and one has a high _____ .

Word Bank

boys

brown

found

house

listen

oil

point

sound

town

voice

Name _____

Vowel Teams ou, ow

You can spell the /ou/ sound with *ou*, as in *mouse*, or *ow*, as in *town*.

▶ Write each basic Spelling Word in the correct column.

Words with ou	Words with ow
_____	_____
_____	_____
_____	_____
_____	_____
_____	_____
_____	_____

Spelling Words
Basic
cow
house
town
shout
down
mouse
found
loud
brown
ground
pound
flower
Review
grew
spoon
boost
threw

Name _____

Vowel Teams ou, ow

The vowel teams *ou* and *ow* can stand for the same sound. They can stand for the vowel sound you hear in the words *out* and *owl*.

▶ Choose and write two words to complete each sentence.

1. A _____ saw a spark on the _____ .

   mount   mouse   loud   ground

2. It ran _____ the forest _____ the alarm.

   around   account   slouching   sounding

3. A _____ of animals heard _____ .

   spouts   crown   crowd   shouts

4. "Stand back _____ !" Bear _____ .

   now   noun   growled   grouch

5. Bear _____ the flame with a _____ .

   scouted   shower   down   doused

6. The animals clap _____ when the flame

   is _____ .

   out   owl   loudly   lousy

Name _____

Vowel Teams ou, ow

You can spell the /ou/ sound with *ou*, as in *house*, or *ow*, as in *cow*.

▶ Read each sentence. Cross out the Spelling Word that is spelled incorrectly. Write it correctly on the line.

1. The mowse ate cheese. _____

2. Walk doun the hill. _____

3. We sat on the growned. _____

4. Have you fownd your toy? _____

5. I live in a small toun. _____

6. A rose is a kind of flour. _____

7. Do not run in the howse. _____

8. That is a lowd horn! _____

9. I used broun paint. _____

▶ Write three sentences with the basic Spelling Words you did not use. Then trade with a partner. Check each other's spelling.

Spelling Words
Basic
cow
house
town
shout
down
mouse
found
loud
brown
ground
pound
flower
Review
grew
spoon
boost
threw

Name _____

Power Words: Draw and Write

Word Bank

| plenty | swipe | whacked | whimpered |

▶ Draw a picture or write words that will help you remember each Power Word from *Jack and the Beanstalk*. Try to write more than you draw.

1. plenty	2. swipe
3. whacked	4. whimpered

Name _____

Figurative Language

Literal language uses words that mean exactly what they say.
Figurative language uses words that mean something different
from what they say. Three types of figurative language are:

- **simile:** compares two different things using the word *like* or *as*

- **idiom:** words that mean something different from their everyday
  meaning

- **alliteration:** a pattern of words with the same first sounds

▶ Answer the questions about *Jack and the Beanstalk.*

🔍 Pages 118–119 How does the simile "held like a treasure" help
you understand how Jack feels about the beans? What does
Jack's mother mean when she says the beans "won't put food
on the table?"

_____

_____

_____

🔍 Pages 124 What does the author mean when she says
Jack "leapt up the beanstalk like a mountain goat"?

_____

_____

_____

Name _____

Phonics Review

- The vowel teams *ou* and *ow* can stand for the vowel sound in *plow* and *proud*. The vowel spellings *oy* and *oi* stand for the vowel sound *joy* and *join*.

- Read longer words one syllable at a time. Use the vowel patterns.

▶ Read the clues. Write the word that answers the clue.

1. I am a name for a light rain.

    shower   **shouter**   **scouting**   _____

2. I tell how a happy child feels.

    jointed   **joyful**   **jousting**   _____

3. I am a name for pants.

    towel   **toilet**   **trousers**   _____

4. I am what you might say if your soup is too hot.

    Couch!   **Ouch!**   **Oil!**   _____

5. I mean that a food is rotten.

    soybeans   **sprouting**   **spoiled**   _____

6. I can spray water.

    flounder   **fountain**   **flower**   _____

Prefix mis-

The **prefix** *mis–* means "wrong." Use the meaning of the prefix and the **base word** to figure out the meaning of the new word. If you are not sure about the meaning of a base word, look it up in a dictionary.

▶ Add the prefix *mis–* to each word. Write the new word on the line. Then write what the word means.

1. mis– + judge = _____ means _____

2. mis– + take = _____ means _____

_____

3. mis– + match = _____ means _____

_____

> **Word Bank**
>
> misled   mispronounce   misuse

▶ Complete each sentence with a word from the box.

4. Did I _____ your name?

5. The directions _____ Juan to believe
   he put the toy together correctly.

6. Because of a _____ on the map, we did not go
   the right way.

Power Words: Yes or No?

Word Bank			
adorable	glanced	hauling	oversized

▶ Read each sentence. Circle **YES** if the word makes sense or **NO** if it does not. Rewrite the sentence so it makes sense.

1. A wagon is good for **hauling** heavy things.

       YES   NO

_____

2. We **glanced** at the picture for a long time.

       YES   NO

_____

3. An **oversized** shirt feels very loose when you put it on.

       YES   NO

_____

4. It is hard to like an **adorable** puppy.

       YES   NO

_____

Name _____

Characters

The **characters** are the people or animals in a story. **External traits** are what a character looks like on the outside. **Internal traits** describe a character's personality, or what he or she thinks and feels.

▶ Answer the questions about *Jackie and the Beanstalk.*

🔍 Pages 134–136 How does Jackie respond when the woman describes the special beans? What does that tell you about Jackie?

_____

_____

_____

_____

🔍 Pages 138–139 How does Jackie feel when she realizes Mr. Fefifofum thinks she stole the harp? Tell how you know. What does she do to feel better? What do these actions tell you about Jackie?

_____

_____

_____

_____

Name _____

Words to Know

Word Bank

also	ball	call	could	every
near	talk	tall	would	year

▶ Circle the word that best completes each sentence.

1. Jess is a (tall, talk) girl.

2. She can (every, also) jump high.

3. She can dunk the (call, ball).

4. She makes it in the hoop almost (every, would) time!

5. (Could, Call) you do that?

6. (Also, Would) you like to try?

7. Jess will (call, talk) her teammates.

8. The team will (talk, would) about the next ball game.

Name _____

Vowel Patterns: /ô/

You can spell the /ô/ sound with *al*, as in *tall*, *aw*, as in *paw*, or *o*, as in *soft*.

► Write each basic Spelling Word in the correct column.

Words with a(l)	Words with aw	Words with o
_____	_____	_____
_____	_____	_____
_____	_____	_____
_____	_____	_____

Spelling Words

Basic

tall

saw

jaw

draw

call

fall

soft

paw

ball

yawn

fog

small

Review

ground

flower

town

loud

Name _____

Vowel Patterns: /ô/

The vowel pattern *aw* stands for the vowel sound in *saw*. The vowel patterns *au*, *al*, *augh*, and *ough* also stand for the same vowel sound.

▶ Write the word that names the picture. Circle the letter or letters that stand for the vowel sound in *saw*.

1. stall   straw   stalk

_____

2. lawful   lawn   launch

_____

3. daughter   drawing   dawn

_____

4. walrus   walled   wrought

_____

5. bawling   bought   baseball

_____

6. seesaw   sawdust   sawhorse

_____

Name _____

Vowel Patterns: /ô/

You can spell the /ô/ sound with *al*, as in *ball*, *aw*, as in *yawn*, or *o*, as in *fog*.

▶ Write the Spelling Word that best completes each sentence.

1. It is hard to see in the _____ .

2. My dog hurt his _____ .

3. Throw the _____ to me.

4. A mouse is very _____ .

5. _____ me on the phone.

6. The pillow is _____ .

7. You chew with your _____ .

8. The pine tree is _____ .

▶ Write four more sentences with missing Spelling Words, like the ones on this page. Then trade with a partner. Complete each other's sentences.

Spelling Words
Basic
tall
saw
jaw
draw
call
fall
soft
paw
ball
yawn
fog
small
Review
ground
flower
town
loud

Power Words: Match

attack	extra	nasty	poke
prickles	sensitive	sharp	thorns

▶ Write the Power Word from *Don't Touch Me!* that best fits each item.

1. This word means the opposite of *pleasant*.

_____

2. Which word means that you give a quick response?

_____

3. A wolf will do this to another animal.

_____

4. Which word means to *jab into suddenly*?

_____

5. When you have more than the usual amount, you have this.

_____

6. An animal will feel pain if it has these stuck in its paw.

_____

7. You should wear gloves when you touch a rose that has these.

_____

8. This word can be used to describe a sewing needle.

_____

Name _____

Text Organization

Text organization is the way an author organizes a text to help readers understand the information. Texts organized by **cause** and **effect** describe how one event leads to another event. A cause is something that happens. An effect is what happens as a result of the cause.

▶ Answer the questions about *Don't Touch Me!*

🔍 Page 147 How does the text help you understand the connection between these plants? What clue does the author give to help you understand the effect of touching these plants?

_____

_____

_____

_____

_____

🔍 Pages 148–149 What causes and effects do you see on these pages? Why did the author organize the selection this way?

_____

_____

_____

_____

Name _____

Phonics Review

The vowel pattern *aw* stands for the vowel sound in *saw*. The vowel patterns *au*, *al*, *augh*, and *ough* can also stand for that sound. The vowel patterns *ear* and *eer* stand for the vowel sound in *hear*.

Read longer words one syllable at a time. Use the vowel patterns.

▶ Choose and write two words to complete each sentence.

1. Paul is _____ of _____ off his bike.

   falling   fawn   fought   fearful

2. The _____ gave me his _____ .

   also   author   awfully   autograph

3. We _____ for the _____ team.

   caused   footrace   cheered   football

4. Mr. Lawton's _____ like to play on the

   _____ .

   daunting   seesaw   sawing   daughters

5. Farmers _____ fill up the _____ .

   awful   always   taught   trough

6. The _____ drops are _____ gone.

   cough   caught   awful   almost

Name _____

Prefix dis-

The **prefix** *dis–* means "not" or "the opposite of." Use the meaning of the prefix and the **base word** to figure out the meaning of the new word. Look up base words you do not know in a dictionary.

▶ Write a word with the prefix *dis–* for each definition.

1. to not approve of: _____

2. to not trust: _____

3. not continued: _____

Word Bank

disbelief	disorder	displeased

▶ Write a word from the box to complete each sentence.

4. The riders were _____ because the bus was late.

5. Too many cooks led to _____ in the kitchen.

6. They gasped with _____ as they watched the magic show.

Name _____

Words to Know

Learn these words. You will see them in your reading and use them in your writing.

▶ Write the word that best completes each sentence.

1. Dave has _____ to do and feels sad.

2. His mom says, "Go play _____ !"

3. Dave plays by _____ in the yard.

4. He _____ wishes for more friends.

5. Grace looks for _____ to play with, too.

6. "_____ we can play tag," Grace says to Dave.

7. "Do not play _____ us!" say Chad and Tess.

8. _____ has fun!

9. "We will play _____ more," says Dave.

10. _____ is more fun with friends!

Word Bank

Everyone

Everything

himself

Maybe

nothing

outside

some

someone

sometimes

without

Name _____

Compound Words

A **compound** word is made up of two shorter words.

pan + cake = pancake

▶ Write each basic Spelling Word in the correct column.

Long vowel in first syllable	Long vowel in second syllable
_____	_____
_____	_____
_____	_____

Others

_____

_____

_____

_____

_____

Spelling Words

Basic

cannot

pancake

maybe

baseball

playground

someone

myself

classroom

sunshine

outside

upon

nothing

Review

small

draw

soft

yawn

Name _____

Prefix pre-

A prefix is a word part added to the beginning of a base word to change its meaning. The prefix *pre–* means "before." The word *precut* begins with the prefix *pre–* and means that something was cut before now.

▶ Choose and write a word to complete each sentence.
Use each word once.

┌─────────────── **Word Bank** ───────────────┐
| prepay   premix   precook   preheat   preorder   prepack |
└───┘

1. The school staff will _____ some food for the bake sale.

2. A teacher wants to _____ Marta's cupcakes.

3. She writes a check to _____ for the cupcakes.

4. Marta can _____ the batter while she waits for Dad.

5. She has to wait for him to _____ the oven.

6. Marta will _____ the teacher's cupcakes first, and then sell the rest.

Name _____

Compound Words

A **compound** word is made up of two shorter words.

    base + ball = baseball

▶ Fill in the missing letters to write a compound word. Then write the Spelling Word on the line.

1. my ___ ___ ___ ___   _____

2. ___ ___ ___ shine   _____

3. ___ ___ ___ ___ ground   _____

4. out ___ ___ ___ ___   _____

5. ___ ___ ___ ___ ball   _____

6. class___ ___ ___ ___   _____

7. may___ ___   _____

8. some___ ___ ___   _____

9. ___ ___ ___ cake   _____

10. ___ ___ on   _____

▶ Write two sentences with the basic Spelling Words you did not use. Then trade with a partner. Check each other's spelling.

Spelling Words
Basic
cannot
pancake
maybe
baseball
playground
someone
myself
classroom
sunshine
outside
upon
nothing
Review
small
draw
soft
yawn

Phonics Review

- A prefix is a syllable added to the beginning of a word to change its meaning. Examples: *pre–* means "before," *re–* means "again," *un–* means "not" or "the opposite," *dis–* means "not."

- The vowel pattern *aw* spells the vowel sound in *saw*. Other vowel patterns for this sound are *au*, *al*, *augh*, and *ough*. The vowel pattern *oo* spells the vowel sound in *moose*. Other vowel patterns for this sound are *o*, *ew*, *ou*, and *ue*.

- Read longer words one syllable at a time. Look for base words, prefixes, endings, and vowel syllable patterns to help you.

▶ Add a prefix to the word in dark print to complete each sentence. Use these prefixes: *pre–*, *dis–*, *un–*, *re–*.

1. Paul **drew** a cartoon for the school paper.

Paul _____ the cartoon because he ripped it.

2. Mr. Hooper **taught** us the song a week before the others.

We ought to sing it best since he _____ it.

3. All but one of the men is **loyal** to the king.

We need to know who the _____ man is.

4. Mr. Brewster **glued** a straw hat onto the scarecrow.

When it rained, the hat came _____ .

Power Words: Match

Word Bank

coast	crouches	flock	mingles
prances	route	trills	wobbly

▶ Write the Power Word from *The Long, Long Journey* that best fits each item.

1. Which word means *moves with high steps*? _____

2. This is another word for *mixes together*. _____

3. It is the path you travel from your house to your school. _____

4. This is another word for how a bird sings. _____

5. Which word means the opposite of *steady*? _____

6. If your friend bends his knees to get low, he does this. _____

7. This is a word that names a large group of birds. _____

8. It is where the ocean meets the land. _____

Words That Name Places

A **noun** is a word that names a person, place, or thing.

Nouns that name places tell where something is happening.

Use a dictionary to find the meaning of nouns you do not know.

▶ Circle the noun that names a place in each word group.

1. sheep   corn   field

2. truck   house   hay

3. farmer   hen   kitchen

4. town   mailbox   deer

5. visitor   airport   child

6. hillside   teacher   peanut

▶ Complete each sentence with a noun that names a place.

7. Many people live in a _____ .

8. We went to the _____
   to read books.

9. When I arrive at _____ ,
   I say hello to my friends.

10. I enjoy spending a day at the _____ .

Name _____

Text Organization

Authors use **text organization** to help readers find information easily.
A text organized by **chronological order** tells about events in order. This
helps readers understand what happened first, next, and last. It also
helps them understand how one event connects to the next.

▶ Answer the questions about *The Long, Long Journey.*

🔍 Pages 170–174 What does the little female learn to do on pages
170–174? In what order does the author describe these events?
Why do you think she did this?

_____

_____

_____

_____

🔍 Pages 176–179 In your own words, tell what happens during
the godwits' long journey. How does the way the text is
organized support the author's purpose for writing?

_____

_____

_____

_____

Context Clues

When you come to a word you do not know, use **context clues** to figure out its meaning. Look around the word you do not know for clues about what it means.

▶ Read each sentence. Circle the clues that help you know the meaning of the underlined word. Then write the meaning on the line.

1. Helen wants to work as a park ranger. She thinks that it will be an exciting career.

_____

2. She uses an axe to hack branches and brush.

_____

3. The towering mountains seem to touch the sky.

_____

4. The paths are hard to see at night. So the workers hold lanterns when they walk on the trails.

_____

Name _____

Digital Reference Sources

You can look up unfamiliar words in a dictionary or glossary. These resources list words in **alphabetical order**. Glossaries or dictionaries may also be **digital resources**, or online tools.

▶ Read the passage. Then answer the questions.

American Bird Migration

Some birds stay close to home. Others travel long distances. Birds that travel are said to *migrate*.

A <u>permanent</u> <u>resident</u> does not migrate at all. You may see those birds all year long.

Birds that migrate a short distance do not go far. They might move up and down a mountain.

Some birds migrate a medium distance. They may <u>span</u> several states as they fly.

Birds that migrate a long distance go far. Some birds may take a long <u>route</u> from the United States to South America.

Name _____

1. Write the underlined words in alphabetical order.

_____

2. Look up *permanent* in a digital dictionary. Write the first meaning you find.

_____

_____

3. Look up *resident* in a digital dictionary. Write the first meaning you find.

_____

_____

4. Which of the underlined words has two possible pronunciations?

_____

5. Look up the word *span* in both a digital and a print dictionary. Compare what you found.

_____

_____

_____

_____

Name _____

Words to Know

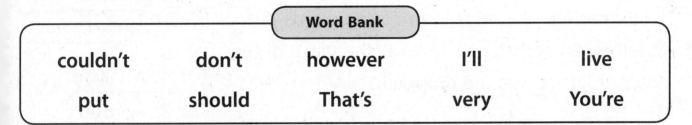

Word Bank				
couldn't	don't	however	I'll	live
put	should	That's	very	You're

▶ Write a word from the box to complete each sentence.

1. I have a _____ loose tooth.

2. It _____ fall out soon.

3. Pat says, "_____ play with it!"

4. "_____ right, Pat," I say.

5. I want to play with it, _____ .

6. _____ lose my tooth very soon.

▶ Write a sentence about what might happen next. Use at least one word from the box.

_____

_____

Name _____

Contractions

A **contraction** is a short form of two words put together. An apostrophe (') takes the place of the letter or letters that are dropped.

do not→don't   it is→it's   I have→I've

▶ Write each basic Spelling Word in the correct box.

Contractions with *not*

_____

_____

_____

_____

Contractions with *is*

_____

_____

_____

Contractions with *have*

_____

_____

_____

Other contractions

_____

_____

_____

Spelling Words

Basic

don't
we'll
it's
I've
didn't
you're
that's
wasn't
you've
who's
they'd
aren't

Review

cannot
maybe
someone
myself

Name _____

Three-Letter Blends

The word *scrape* begins with three consonant letters. It is a three-letter blend. You say and blend each consonant sound closely together to read the word. The word *throat* begins with a three-letter blend, but you say two sounds for it.

▶ Look at the picture and read the question. Write the answer.

Is it **spring** or **string**?

_____

Do you use it to **squint** or **sprint**?

_____

Do you use it to **strum** or **scrub**?

_____

Can you **throw** it or **scroll** it?

_____

Do you **thread** it or **spread** it?

_____

Are they **stretchy** or **scratchy**?

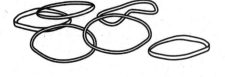

_____

Name _____

Contractions

A **contraction** is a short form of two words put together. An apostrophe (') takes the place of the letter or letters that are dropped.

did not→didn't   that is→that's   you have→you've

▶ Put the words together to form a contraction. Write the Spelling Word on the line.

1. are + not = _____

2. did + not = _____

3. who + is = _____

4. was + not = _____

5. you + have = _____

6. I + have = _____

7. do + not = _____

8. it + is = _____

9. you + are = _____

10. we + will = _____

▶ Write two sentences with the basic Spelling Words you did not use. Then trade with a partner. Check each other's spelling.

Spelling Words
Basic
don't
we'll
it's
I've
didn't
you're
that's
wasn't
you've
who's
they'd
aren't
Review
cannot
maybe
someone
myself

Name _____

Power Words: Draw and Write

attached	crack	surface	wraps

▶ Draw a picture or write words that will help you remember each Power Word from *Sea Otter Pups*. Try to write more than you draw.

1. attached	2. crack
3. surface	4. wraps

Name _____

Text Features

Authors may use different text features to organize information. This makes the information easier for the reader to find or understand. **Captions** give information about pictures. **Labels** name the parts of a picture. **Headings** tell what a page or section of a text is about. **Graphics** are visual features that include pictures, symbols, and **maps**.

▶ Answer the questions about *Sea Otter Pups*.

🔍 Page 187 What do the heading and labels on this page tell you?

_____

_____

_____

🔍 Page 188 Why are there two maps, and what is the purpose of the yellow highlighting?

_____

_____

_____

_____

_____

_____

Name _____

Phonics Review

- The word *scrape* begins with a three-letter blend. You blend each consonant sound closely together to say the word. The word *throat* begins with a three-letter blend, but you say two sounds for it.

- A contraction is a shorter way of saying two words together. An apostrophe (') takes the place of one or more letters. The word *can't* is a contraction for *can not*. Here are more examples: *we'll = we will, you're = you are, they've = they have, he's = he is.*

- Here are special contractions: *don't = do not, won't = will not.*

▶ Chose and write two words to complete each sentence.

1. Dean _____ _____ the toothpaste.

   can't   isn't   squeeze   splurge

2. _____ got a _____ in my finger.

   I've   Don't   splinter   splatter

3. _____ going to _____ a class party.

   Won't   We're   throw   throat

4. We _____ won, but I _____ out.

   shouldn't   should've   streak   struck

5. _____ _____ the pots clean.

   She's   She'll   scrubbing   scratching

Name _____

Prefix *mis-*

Add a **prefix** to the beginning of a **base word** to change its meaning. The prefix *mis–* means "wrong." Use a dictionary to find the meaning of base words that you do not know.

▶ Add the prefix *mis–* to each base word. Then write a sentence using the new word.

1. **spell** _____

_____

_____

2. **use** _____

_____

_____

_____

3. **counted** _____

_____

_____

4. **read** _____

_____

_____

Name _____

Power Words: Yes or No?

| Word Bank |
| hide   sheltered   weary   wit |

▶ Read each sentence. Circle **YES** if the word makes sense or **NO** if it does not. Rewrite the sentence so it makes sense.

1. A rabbit has a furry **hide**.

   YES   NO

_____

2. An open area is a **sheltered** place to wait during a storm.

   YES   NO

_____

_____

3. If you feel **weary**, you do not need to rest.

   YES   NO

_____

4. A person with **wit** does not act funny.

   YES   NO

Name _____

Elements of Poetry

Poetry is a special kind of writing. The words in poems create pictures and make music. **Rhythm** gives the words in poems a beat. **Rhyme** happens when words end with the same sounds. **Repetition** is when the same words or lines appear over and over. Poets often use **descriptive language** to help readers picture what they are writing about.

▶ Answer the questions about *At Home in the Wild*.

🔍 Pages 202–203 What do you notice about which words rhyme in the first two stanzas? Why do you think the poet did this? Why do you think the poet used repeating lines in the poem?

_____

_____

_____

_____

🔍 Pages 204–206 Why do you think each verse begins with the same phrase? What do you notice about the second line in each verse?

_____

_____

_____

Name _____

Words to Know

<table>
<tr><td colspan="5" align="center">**Word Bank**</td></tr>
<tr><td>above</td><td>again</td><td>along</td><td>myself</td><td>once</td></tr>
<tr><td>piece</td><td>something</td><td>table</td><td>they</td><td>wanted</td></tr>
</table>

▶ Circle the word that best completes each sentence.

1. Sue put a pie on the (table, along).

2. She cut a (something, piece) of pie.

3. "I will eat this piece (above, myself)," she said.

4. "I (again, wanted) to eat some pie, too," said Jack.

5. Sue cut into the pie (again, table).

6. (Something, They) both ate big pieces of pie.

7. They feel full (once, along) they are done.

Name _____

Soft g (-ge, -dge)

You can spell the soft *g*, or /j/, sound with the letters
-ge, as in *cage*, or *-dge*, as in *judge*.

▶ Write each basic Spelling Word in the correct
column.

Words with -ge	Words with -dge
_____	_____
_____	_____
_____	_____
_____	_____
_____	_____
_____	_____

Spelling Words

Basic

bridge

huge

stage

judge

cage

pledge

badge

fudge

dodge

edge

age

lodge

Review

I've

didn't

you're

they'd

Name _____

Consonant + *le*

The word *little* has two syllables: *lit-tle*. The first syllable is closed. It has a short vowel sound. The last syllable is a consonant + *le* syllable. It has a quiet vowel sound.

▶ Choose and write the word that names the picture. Circle the consonant + *le* syllable.

fizzle fiddle fumble	**baffles bobbles bubbles**

_____	_____
kettle kibble knuckle	**goggles giggles grapples**

_____	_____
cuddle candle crinkle	**ripple rumble rattle**

_____	_____

Name _____

Soft g (–ge, –dge)

You can spell the soft *g*, or /j/, sound with the letters –*ge*, as in *age*, or –*dge*, as in *badge*.

▶ Write the Spelling Word that best completes each sentence.

1. Mom made a tray of _____ .

2. Clean the pet's _____ .

3. We walked over the _____ .

4. A whale is _____ !

5. You can vote at _____ 18.

6. Don't stand by the cliff's _____ !

7. We ran to _____ the ball.

8. Who will _____ the art show?

9. The actors are on the _____ .

10. A police officer has a _____ .

▶ Write two more sentences with missing Spelling Words, like the ones on this page. Then trade with a partner. Complete each other's sentences.

Spelling Words
Basic
bridge
huge
stage
judge
cage
pledge
badge
fudge
dodge
edge
age
lodge
Review
I've
didn't
you're
they'd

Name _____

Power Words: Match

Word Bank

arrive	growled	grumpy	joking
offered	shrugged	stubborn	tucked

▶ Write the Power Word from *Abuelo and the Three Bears* that best fits each item.

1. When you say something to be funny, you are doing this. _____

2. This word describes someone who is in a bad mood. _____

3. Which word means *reach* or *come to*? _____

4. When someone does not want to change, they are this. _____

5. This is what you did when you asked a friend if you could help. _____

6. If a dog did this, you would want to stay away. _____

7. Which word means *pushed behind or into*? _____

8. When I didn't know the answer to my friend's question, I did this. _____

Name _____

Figurative Language

Literal language means just what it says. **Figurative language** uses words in different ways. It makes writing colorful and interesting. An **idiom** is a phrase that means something different from its everyday meaning. A **hyperbole** is a statement that is so crazy it can't be true.

▶ Answer the questions about *Abuelo and the Three Bears*.

🔍 Page 217 If you are so hungry that you could eat an elephant, how hungry are you? Why does the author use hyperbole?

_____

_____

_____

_____

🔍 Page 220 Abuelo says that Trencitas "followed her nose." What does this idiom mean? Explain why the idiom has this meaning.

_____

_____

_____

_____

_____

Phonics Review

You can use syllable patterns to read longer words. Look at the syllables in bold print to learn about syllable patterns:

- *candle*, **can**-*dle*: closed syllable CVC pattern for a short vowel sound
- *candle*, *can*-**dle**: consonant + *le* pattern for a soft vowel sound
- *bonus*, **bo**-*nus*: open syllable CV pattern for a long vowel sound
- *carpet*, **car**-*pet*: r-controlled vowel sound syllable
- *awful*, **aw**-*ful* and *teabag*, **tea**-*bag*: vowel team syllables

▶ Choose and write two words to complete each sentence.

1. My _____ barks when I play the _____ .

     bugle   **bacon**   **beacon**   **beagle**

2. The coins _____ in my _____ pocket.

     joyful   **jingle**   **jacket**   **jungle**

3. Mom put a vase of _____ on the _____ .

     tulips   **tumbles**   **table**   **turtle**

4. A jigsaw _____ is _____ for a rainy day.

     pebble   **pickle**   **perfect**   **puzzle**

5. Jim likes _____ _____ in his notebook.

     drawing   **dropping**   **drizzle**   **doodles**

6. Silly _____ make Dad _____ .

     cartons   **cartoons**   **chuckle**   **checker**

Name _____

Prefix pre-

Add a **prefix** in front of a **base word** to change the meaning of the word. The prefix *pre-* means "before." If you do not know the meaning of a base word, look the word up in a dictionary.

▶ Add the prefix *pre-* to each word. Then write the meaning of the new word.

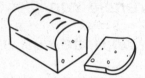

1. sliced: _____

2. cook: _____

3. paid: _____

4. measure: _____

5. package: _____

▶ Choose two words with the prefix *pre-* from above and write a sentence for each. Check the meaning of base words you do not know in a dictionary.

6. _____

_____ .

7. _____

_____ .

Name _____

Words to Know

Knowing how to read and write these words can make you a better reader and writer.

Word Bank

| against | cover | early | getting | here |
| hurry | much | stopped | toward | your |

▶ Circle the word that best completes each sentence.

1. Molly was in a (hurry, cover).

2. She had to get to the park (early, toward).

3. Her team had a game (much, against) Paul and his team.

4. Her mom (toward, stopped) the car at a red light.

5. "We don't have (your, much) time," said Molly.

6. Mom drove the car (getting, toward) the park.

7. "You're (here, cover)!" said Paul. "Let's play!"

▶ Write a sentence to tell what happens next. Use a word from the box that you did not circle.

_____

_____

Name _____

Inflections –ed, –ing

When you add –ed or –ing to some base words, you change their spelling. When a base word has a short vowel followed by one consonant, double the consonant and add –ed or –ing.

run + n + ing = running   clap + p + ed = clapped

▶ Write each basic Spelling Word in the correct column.

Words with –ing	Words with –ed
_____	_____
_____	_____
_____	_____
_____	_____
_____	_____
_____	_____

Spelling Words

Basic

running

clapped

stopped

hopping

batted

selling

pinned

cutting

sitting

rubbed

missed

grabbed

Review

stage

badge

huge

lodge

Prefix mis-

A prefix is a word part added to the beginning of a word to change its meaning. The word *misspell* begins with the prefix *mis-*. The prefix *mis-* means "bad, badly" or "wrong, wrongly." *Misspell* means a word is not spelled correctly.

▶ Write the word in dark print with the prefix *mis-* to complete each sentence.

1. Matt **counted** the cups and plates for the party.

   He _____ and had to count them again.

2. Ann **deals** seven cards to each player.

   She _____ and gives Dan only six cards.

3. The clerk **charged** Meg for two books.

   Meg got one book so the clerk _____ her.

4. Benny **matched** all the clean socks for Mom.

   He _____ a dark blue sock with a black sock.

5. Mrs. Summers **led** June to think that Gram was not coming.

   She _____ June, so Gram's visit was a surprise.

Name _____

Inflections –ed, –ing

When you add *–ed* or *–ing* to some base words, you change their spelling. When a base word has a short vowel followed by one consonant, double the consonant and add *–ed* or *–ing*.

cut + **t** + ing = cutting   bat + **t** + ed = batted

▶ Fill in the missing letters to write a Spelling Word. Then write the Spelling Word on the line.

1. cla ___ ___ ed   _____

2. mi ___ ___ ed   _____

3. ru ___ ___ ing   _____

4. gra ___ ___ ed   _____

5. sto ___ ___ ed   _____

6. cu ___ ___ ing   _____

7. ho ___ ___ ing   _____

8. se ___ ___ ing   _____

9. si ___ ___ ing   _____

10. ba ___ ___ ed   _____

▶ Write two sentences with the basic Spelling Words you did not use. Then trade with a partner. Check each other's spelling.

Spelling Words

Basic

running
clapped
stopped
hopping
batted
selling
pinned
cutting
sitting
rubbed
missed
grabbed

Review

stage
badge
huge
lodge

Phonics Review

- A prefix is a word part added to the beginning of a base word to change its meaning. Examples: *pre–* = "before," *re–* = "again," *un–* = "not" or "the opposite," *dis–* = "not."

- A suffix is a word part added to the end of a base word to change its meaning. Examples: *–ly* = "in that way," *–y* = "like," *–less* = "without," *–ful* = "full of," *–er* compares two things, *–est* compares three or more things.

- Read longer words one syllable at a time. Look for base words, prefixes, endings, and vowel syllable patterns to help you.

▶ Choose a word from the box to complete each sentence.

> **Word Bank**
>
> breathless   displeased   misspelled   quickly   reread   thankful

1. Alex _____ his report to look for mistakes.

2. He saw a _____ word on the last page.

3. Alex was _____ with himself.

4. He was _____ he still had time to fix it.

5. Alex fixed the mistake and _____ ran to the bus stop.

6. He was still _____ when the bus pulled up.

Power Words: Match

```
                    ┌─── Word Bank ───┐
  darting      delight      fragrant      grunted

  hollered      nod        slippery      smothered
```

▶ Write the Power Word from *Where on Earth Is My Bagel?*
that best fits each item.

1. When the bear made a low, deep
sound, it did this.   _____

2. This movement of your head means
you agree.   _____

3. Which word means *great joy*?   _____

4. This word means the same as
shouted loudly.   _____

5. This is how something that is
smooth and wet feels.   _____

6. Which word means *moving quickly
from place to place*?   _____

7. What is it called when food is
thickly covered in a sauce?   _____

8. Which word means the opposite
of *stinky*?   _____

Suffixes –ion, –tion, –sion

A **suffix** is a word part added to the end of a **base word**. It changes the meaning of the word. The suffixes *–ion*, *–tion*, and *–sion* mean "an act of," "a condition of," or "the result of." Use a dictionary to look up the meaning of base words you do not know.

Word Bank

celebration	confusion	hibernation
instruction	prediction	separation

▶ Choose the word from the box that best matches each definition. Write the word on the line.

1. the act of celebrating something   _____

2. the act of predicting the future   _____

3. the condition of not understanding   _____

4. the condition of hibernating   _____

5. the act of instructing   _____

6. the result of separating   _____

Name _____

Theme

The **theme** of a story is the big idea, **moral**, or lesson the author wants readers to take away. To find the theme, identify the **topic**, or what the story is mostly about. Next look for evidence to figure out the message the author wants you to learn. Say the theme in your own words.

▶ Answer the questions about *Where on Earth Is My Bagel?*

🔍 Pages 247–251 Who is the story's main character, and what problem does he have? How does Yum Yung try to solve his problem?

_____

_____

_____

_____

🔍 Pages 260–264 What does Yum Yung realize about where he can get a bagel? Use evidence from the text to explain your answer. What theme, or big idea, does this help you figure out?

_____

_____

_____

_____

Shades of Meaning

Shades of meaning are the small differences in meaning between words that are **synonyms**, or mean the same thing.

```
Word Bank

        angry                                    delighted
```

▶ Fill in each blank with a synonym from the box.

1. **(least)** _____ **(greatest)**

   happy   pleased   _____

2. **(least)** _____ **(greatest)**

   upset   _____   furious

```
Word Bank

    peek                    look                    watch
```

▶ Put the words in order, from least to greatest. Then complete each sentence.

_____

3. I _____ at my teacher when she is talking.

4. Cover your eyes, and don't _____ !

5. We will _____ the movie together.

Name _____

Follow a Research Plan

A research plan is a list of steps to follow to do a research project. Follow these steps:

1. Select a topic.

2. Ask questions about the topic.

3. Pick resources to use for your research.

4. Keep a record of the resources you use to avoid **plagiarism**, or copying another person's work without giving credit.

5. Organize the information.

6. Decide how you want to share the information.

7. Present the information.

Research Prompt: Think about something from *Where on Earth Is My Bagel?* that you would like to know more about. Create a research plan that will help you complete your research project.

1. Write your topic: I would like to learn more about

_____.

2. Write three research questions about the topic. What do you want to know?

1. _____

2. _____

3. _____

Name _____

3. Pick your sources. Look for answers to your research questions. Write the information you find in your sources.

_____

_____

_____

4. Keep a record of the resources you use. Write the titles and names of authors in the chart.

Record of My Sources	
Title	Author's Name

5. Organize the information you found. Tell what you learned.

1. _____

2. _____

3. _____

6. How will you share your information? Circle one or two.

writing   drawing   talking

Name _____

Words to Know

▶ Write the word that best completes each sentence.

1. Seth likes _____ to the jungle.

2. Rich always _____ with him.

3. Squawk! They hear birds in the _____ .

4. The sounds are _____ from the tree.

5. Seth sees a nest _____ the ground.

6. _____ is a huge beetle on the path.

7. It walks _____ the tree.

8. _____ knows what they will see next?

▶ Write a sentence for a word from the box you did not write yet.

Word Bank
area
around
coming
from
goes
going
second
seemed
there
who

_____

_____

_____

Name _____

Inflections –ed, –ing

When you add *–ed* or *–ing* to some base words, you change their spelling. When a base word ends in *e*, drop the *e* and add *–ed* or *–ing*.

like – **e** + ed = liked   ride – **e** + ing = riding

▶ Write each basic Spelling Word in the correct column.

Words with –ed	Words with –ing
_____	_____
_____	_____
_____	_____
_____	_____
_____	_____

Spelling Words
Basic
liked
using
riding
chased
spilled
making
closed
hoping
baked
hiding
standing
asked
Review
hopping
clapped
pinned
cutting

Name _____

Open and Closed Syllables

A closed syllable has a short vowel sound. An open syllable has a long vowel sound. Divide a longer word into syllables to read it:

- VC/CV pattern: Divide between the consonants, *kitten = kit/ten*.

- V/CV pattern: Divide after the long vowel, *minus = mi/nus*.

- Rule breakers: If a word does not sound right with a long vowel, divide after the consonant and try a short vowel, *wagon = wag/on*.

▶ Draw a line (/) to divide each word into syllables.

h e r o	r i b b o n	p r o b l e m
h o t e l	m e n u	p i c n i c

▶ Use the words above to complete the sentences.

1. Greg got each math _____ right.

2. The family stayed in a _____ with a pool.

3. Who is your favorite super _____ ?

4. What will you order from the _____ ?

5. Mom put a _____ on the gift.

6. A sunny day is a good day for a _____ .

Name _____

Inflections –ed, –ing

When you add *–ed* or *–ing* to some base words, you change their spelling. When a base word ends in *e*, drop the *e* and add *–ed* or *–ing*.

close – **e** + ed = closed   hide – **e** + ing = hiding

▶ Read each sentence. Cross out the Spelling Word that is spelled incorrectly. Write it correctly on the line.

1. Where is he hidding?   _____

2. Dad is makeing dinner.   _____

3. I like ridding my bike.   _____

4. Pat clossed the door.   _____

5. Jan is useing the pen.   _____

6. The dog chassed the cat.   _____

7. Who spild the milk?   _____

8. Ben bakked a pie.   _____

9. He likd the meal.   _____

▶ Write three sentences with the basic Spelling Words you did not use. Then trade with a partner. Check each other's spelling.

Spelling Words
Basic
liked
using
riding
chased
spilled
making
closed
hoping
baked
hiding
standing
asked
Review
hopping
clapped
pinned
cutting

Name _____

Power Words: Yes or No?

Word Bank

| clutched | forgot | races | trunk |

▶ Read each sentence. Circle **YES** if the word makes sense or
NO if it does not. Rewrite the sentence so it makes sense.

1. A squirrel is an animal that **races** up and down
    the **trunk** of a tree.

    YES   NO

    _____

2. Meg **clutched** her friend's arm so that she could fall down.

    YES   NO

    _____

    _____

3. Peter came to the party because Rachel **forgot** to invite him.

    YES   NO

    _____

    _____

Name _____

Central Idea

The **topic** of a text is the person or thing that text is mostly about. The **central idea** is the most important idea about the topic. Readers can use **supporting evidence**, or details, facts, and examples, to figure out the central idea.

▶ Answer the questions about *May Day Around the World.*

🔍 Pages 270–271 What is this text mostly about? How do you know?

_____

_____

_____

🔍 Pages 272–274 What details in this part of the text give more information about May Day celebrations? What central idea do these details support?

_____

_____

_____

_____

_____

_____

Name _____

Phonics Review

Divide a longer word into syllables to read it:

- VCCCV pattern: Divide before the consonant + *le*, *tumble = tum / ble, puzzle = puz / zle.*

- VC/CV pattern: Divide between the consonants, *mitten = mit/ten.*

- V/CV pattern: Divide after the long vowel, *bonus = bo/nus.*

- Rule breakers: If a word does not sound right with a long vowel, divide after the consonant and try a short vowel, *seven = sev/en.*

▶ Read each sentence. Write each word with two syllables. Then draw a line (/) between the two syllables.

1. Jan had a dance solo in the school program.

    _____   _____

2. The strap on the saddle is broken.

    _____   _____

3. The rabbit ran a zigzag path to the tree.

    _____   _____

4. Gail ate an apple muffin for a snack.

    _____   _____

5. When Beth giggles, her dimples show.

    _____   _____

Suffixes -y, -ly

Add a **suffix** to the end of a **base word** to change its meaning. The suffix –y means, "having or being like something." The suffix –ly explains how or when something is done.

▶ Add –y or –ly to the base word to make a new word. Write the new word and its meaning on the line.

1. snow + y = _____ : _____

2. quick + ly = _____ : _____

3. dirt + y _____ : _____

```
                        Definition Bank
```

in a silly or foolish way	**in a confident way**
being cold	**having a lot of grease**

▶ Choose the definition from the box that matches each word. Write it on the line. Circle *adjective* if the word is a describing word. Circle *adverb* if the word tells how or when.

4. chilly: _____   adjective   adverb

5. foolishly: _____   adjective   adverb

6. greasy: _____   adjective   adverb

7. confidently: _____   adjective   adverb

Name _____

Power Words: Draw and Write

| final | founded | imaginary | patient |

▶ Draw a picture or write words that will help you remember each Power Word from *Goal!* Try to write more than you draw.

1. final

2. founded

3. imaginary

4. patient

Name _____

Central Idea

The **topic** of a text is the person or thing that text is mostly about. The **central idea** is the most important idea about the topic. You can figure out the central idea by looking for **supporting evidence**—details, facts, or examples in the text—that tells about the central idea.

▶ Answer the questions about *Goal!*

🔍 Pages 280–281 What is the topic of this text? What evidence helps you identify the topic? What do details in this part of the text help you understand about the topic?

_____

_____

_____

_____

🔍 Pages 286–288 What important idea about soccer does the author share with readers? What supporting evidence helps you understand the central idea?

_____

_____

_____

_____

Name _____

Words to Know

Word Bank				
ago	carry	many	money	only
ride	sky	study	wasn't	world

▶ Read the clues below. Write the correct word from the Word Bank.

1. Planes fly in the _____ .   _____

2. What to do for a test   _____

3. Was + not   _____

4. Coins   _____

5. A long time _____ …   _____

6. More than a few   _____

7. I _____ in the truck.   _____

8. Where we live   _____

Name _____

Long e (y)

You can spell the long e sound with *y*, as in *puppy*.

▶ Write each basic Spelling Word in the correct column.

Words with 2 consonants before *y*	Words with 1 consonant before *y*
_____	_____
_____	_____
_____	_____
_____	_____
_____	_____
_____	_____
_____	_____

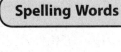

Spelling Words

Basic

pretty
baby
very
puppy
funny
carry
lucky
only
sunny
penny
plenty
twenty

Review

standing
hoping
spilled
using

Name _____

Long a, e

- There are many spellings for long *a* and long *e*. The words *vein* and *they* have the long *a* vowel teams *ei* and *ey*.

- The vowel team *ey* can also spell the long *e* sound, as in *key*. The letter *y* sometimes acts as a vowel. It stands for the long *e* at the end of words with two syllables, as in *baby*.

▶ Choose and write the word that answers the clue.

sleigh	city	prey	money	neighbor	chilly

1. This is a person who lives near you. _____

2. This is what an animal hunts. _____

3. This is what you might save in a bank. _____

4. This is a thing you might ride in
   the snow. _____

5. This place is bigger than a town. _____

6. This word means you are a little cold. _____

Name _____

Long e (y)

You can spell the long *e* sound with *y*, as in *sunny*.

▶ Write the Spelling Word that best completes each sentence.

1. Min told a _____ joke.

2. We have _____ of time.

3. The fire is _____ hot.

4. That is a _____ rose.

5. The _____ is in the crib.

6. Our _____ barks a lot!

7. Dean is _____ years old.

8. There is _____ one apple left.

9. One _____ is one cent.

10. The day is hot and _____ .

▶ Write two more sentences with missing Spelling Words, like the ones on this page. Then trade with a partner. Complete each other's sentences.

Spelling Words
Basic
pretty
baby
very
puppy
funny
carry
lucky
only
sunny
penny
plenty
twenty
Review
standing
hoping
spilled
using

Power Words: Match

```
┌──────────────────── Word Bank ────────────────────┐
│   adventures      breathless      clamber      flitting   │
│     leave           mound          shuffled      stacked   │
└────────────────────────────────────────────────────┘
```

▶ Write the Power Word from *Poems in the Attic* that best fits each item.

1. This is how you walked when you dragged your feet.   _____

2. How would you feel right after you ran many laps?   _____

3. Which word describes a place that is filled up with something?   _____

4. This is time away from work.   _____

5. Which word has the same meaning as *hill* or *pile*?   _____

6. This is how you are moving when you climb quickly.   _____

7. Which word describes how a bird or butterfly is moving?   _____

8. These are exciting experiences.   _____

Name _____

Story Structure

Most stories have the same **story structure.** The **conflict,** or problem, the characters face is introduced in the beginning. In the middle of the story, **events** happen as characters try to solve the conflict. At the end of the story, events explain the **resolution,** or how the conflict is solved. The conflict, events, and resolution make up the story's **plot.**

▶ Answer the questions about *Poems in the Attic.*

🔍 Pages 294–301 What events happen in the beginning of the story? Use details from the poems to help you. What challenge does the girl face now that Mama once faced, too?

_____

_____

_____

_____

🔍 Pages 308–310 How do the girl's story and Mama's story end? Use evidence to explain how each had their conflict resolved.

_____

_____

_____

_____

Phonics Review

- One spelling for long *a* is the VC*e* pattern, as in *cake*. The letter *a* spells long *a* in open syllables, as in *bacon*. The vowel teams *ai, ay, ei*, and *ey* also spell long *a*.

- One spelling for long *e* is the VC*e* pattern, as in *these*. The letter *e* spells long *e* in open syllables, as in *me*. The vowel teams *ee, ea*, and *ey* can spell long *e*. So can the letter *y* at the end of words with two syllables, as in *funny*.

- Read longer words one syllable at a time. Look for base words, prefixes, endings, and vowel syllable patterns to help you.

▶ Choose and write the word that completes the sentence.

1. The _____ in the sky has many colors.

   rainbow   **reindeer**   **restless**

2. Bees make sweet _____ in a hive.

   heavy   **honey**   **happy**

3. To play the game right, _____ the rules.

   oily   **only**   **obey**

4. The horse is _____ for carrots.

   neighing   **neighbor**   **naming**

5. I can rock the baby in the _____ .

   candle   **cradle**   **creeping**

6. My feet get _____ when I walk on the beach.

   silly   **survey**   **sandy**

Name _____

Suffixes –ion, –tion, –sion

A **suffix** is a word part added to the end of a base word that
changes the meaning of the word. The suffixes –ion, –tion, and
–sion mean "an act of," "a condition of," or "the result of."

▶ Write the meaning of each base word. Use the base word
and suffix to determine the meaning of each new word.
Look up base words you do not know in a dictionary.

Base Word and Meaning	Suffix	New Word	Meaning
1. illustrate _____	–ion	illustration	
2. expand _____ _____	–sion	expansion	
3. reproduce _____	–tion	reproduction	

▶ Underline the suffix, and write the meaning of the new word
on the line. You may use a dictionary to look up the base word.

4. election: _____

Name _____

Words to Know

Learn these words. You will see them in your reading and use them in your writing.

Word Bank

brother	happened	happy	help	home
mama	papa	sister	suddenly	surprise

▶ Write a word from the box to complete each sentence.

1. Jack is my baby _____ .

2. He played with his blocks and was _____ .

3. But then Jack _____ started to cry!

4. My big _____ Tara came into the room.

5. "How can I _____ ?" she asked.

6. "Let's see what _____ ," I said.

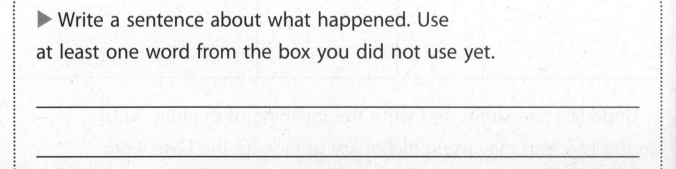

▶ Write a sentence about what happened. Use at least one word from the box you did not use yet.

_____

_____

Name _____

Suffixes –ly, –ful, –er, –est

You can add a **suffix**, or ending, to a base word to change the word's meaning. Some suffixes are –ly, –ful, –er, and –est.

week + ly = weekly   thank + ful = thankful
long + er = longer   young + est = youngest

▶ Write each basic Spelling Word in the correct box.

Words with –ly	Words with –ful
_____	_____
_____	_____
_____	_____
_____	_____
_____	_____

Words with –er	Words with –est
_____	_____
_____	_____

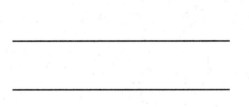

Spelling Words

Basic

youngest
hopeful
fairest
weekly
thankful
wishful
kindly
longer
lighter
painful
mouthful
weakly

Review

lucky
carry
only
sunny

Vowel Team Syllables

Two or more letters together can form a vowel team. In a vowel team syllable, the letters stand for one vowel sound. The word *heating* has two syllables: *heat/ing*. The first syllable has a long *e* vowel team, *ea*. It is a vowel team syllable.

▶ Read each word. Then write the word and draw a line to separate the syllables.

higher _____	bowlful _____
prepaid _____	seedless _____
drawing _____	upload _____

▶ Choose and write a word from above to complete each sentence. You will not use all the words.

1. Dad _____ for the tickets online.

2. Many grapes have tiny seeds or are _____ .

3. June made a _____ of trail mix for the party.

4. The plane climbed _____ into the sky.

5. I used magnets to put my _____ on the fridge.

Name _____

Suffixes -*ly*, -*ful*, -*er*, -*est*

You can add a **suffix**, or ending, to a base word to change the word's meaning. Some suffixes are -*ly*, -*ful*, -*er*, and -*est*.

kind + ly = kindly   mouth + ful = mouthful
light + er = lighter   fair + est = fairest

▶ Write the missing letters. Then write the Spelling Word on the line.

1. fair _____   _____

2. mouth _____   _____

3. kind _____   _____

4. long _____   _____

5. thank _____   _____

6. young _____   _____

7. wish _____   _____

8. week _____   _____

9. light _____   _____

10. hope _____   _____

▶ Write two sentences with the basic Spelling Words you did not use. Be sure to check your spelling.

Spelling Words
Basic
youngest
hopeful
fairest
weekly
thankful
wishful
kindly
longer
lighter
painful
mouthful
weakly
Review
lucky
carry
only
sunny

Phonics Review

You can read longer words by looking for syllable patterns.

- VC/CV pattern has two vowel spellings separated by two consonants. Divide between the consonants: *helmet* = hel/met.

- V/CV pattern has two vowel spellings separated by one consonant. Divide after the first vowel spelling: *silent* = si/lent, *teacup* = tea/cup.

- VCCCV pattern has two vowel spellings separated by three consonants. Divide the consonants so that blends or digraphs stay together: *unblock* = un/block, *speechless* = speech/less.

▶ Read each sentence. Write the words that have more than one syllable. Draw lines (/) to separate the syllables.

1. The pilot did a preflight check of the plane.

   _____   _____

2. Max injured his leg and limped painfully home.

   _____   _____

3. That speaker gave a hiss that made it difficult to hear.

   _____   _____

4. Mom is repainting the bathroom.

   _____   _____

Name _____

Words to Know

▶ Write the word that best completes each sentence.

1. The _____ is high in the sky.

2. Amy and Joe go outside _____
   it is a nice day.

3. They _____ some flowers in
   the garden.

4. Amy digs into the _____ .

5. Then Joe puts the _____ sprout
   in the hole.

6. We need _____ to make the
   ground wet and help the plants grow.

7. Amy and Joe put _____ their tools.

8. What _____ will they do today?

Word Bank

away

because

country

earth

else

green

plant

rain

sea

sun

Grade 2

299

Module 11 • Week 2

Name _____

Prefixes un-, re-, dis-

You can add a **prefix** to the beginning of a base word to change the word's meaning. Some prefixes are *un-*, *re-*, and *dis-*.

> un + lock = unlock   re + read = reread
> dis + like = dislike

▶ Write each basic Spelling Word in the correct column.

Words with un-	Words with re-	Words with dis-
_____	_____	_____
_____	_____	_____
_____	_____	_____
_____	_____	_____
_____		

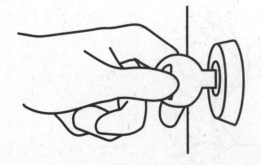

| Spelling Words |

Basic

uncover

retell

untangle

repaint

refill

dislike

distrust

unzip

reread

unable

unlock

replay

Review

thankful

kindly

hopeful

weakly

r-Controlled Vowel Syllables

When the letter *r* follows a vowel, it often changes the way the vowel sounds. Listen for the *r*-controlled vowel sounds in these words: *dark, port, girl, hurt, fern*. When you divide a longer word with an *r*-controlled vowel into syllables, the vowel and the *r* always stay together.

▶ Read each word. Then write the word and draw a line to separate the syllables.

sharpest _____	thirteen _____
report _____	blurry _____
party _____	turnips _____

▶ Choose and write a word from above to complete each sentence. You will not use all the words.

1. The photo was _____ , so I retook it.

2. The saw is the _____ tool in the shed.

3. Marcus will turn _____ next week.

4. Rob wrote a _____ about sea turtles.

5. Did Gram add _____ to the stew?

Name _____

Prefixes un-, re-, dis-

You can add a **prefix** to the beginning of a base word to change the word's meaning. Some prefixes are *un-*, *re-*, and *dis-*.

un + zip = unzip   re + tell = retell
dis + trust = distrust

▶ Add the correct prefix to each base word to form a Spelling Word. Write the Spelling Word on the line.

1. Hal will _____ **read** the book. _____

2. Please _____ **tangle** my laces. _____

3. The pets _____ **like** loud sounds. _____

4. She will _____ **paint** the room. _____

5. Can you _____ **lock** the door? _____

6. He may _____ **cover** clues. _____

7. Julia can _____ **play** the movie. _____

8. Mom will _____ **zip** her bag. _____

▶ Write two more sentences like these. Then trade with a partner. Complete each other's sentences.

Name _____

Phonics Review

When the letter *r* follows a vowel, it often changes the vowel sound. Listen for the *r*-controlled vowel sounds in these words: *art*, *cork*, *dirt*, *turn*, *verb*.

To read longer words, look for vowel and syllable patterns. The word *restarted* has three syllables: *re/start/ed*. It has the prefix *re–*, the *r*-controlled vowel syllable *start*, and the ending *–ed*. Blend each syllable. Then connect the syllables to read the word.

▶ Read each sentence. Write the words that have more than one syllable. Draw lines (/) to separate the syllables.

1. The class is performing a play about a seahorse.

   _____   _____

2. Did Jay remember to record the sports show last night?

   _____   _____

3. Salt and pepper will help to flavor the rice dish.

   _____   _____

4. John had forgotten to mail the postcard.

   _____   _____

5. The vet firmly held the squirming cat.

   _____   _____

Name _____

Words to Know

Word Bank

bed	enough	family	list	oh
people	shop	sleep	today	tomorrow

▶ Circle the word that best completes each sentence.

1. My (family, tomorrow) is going on a trip.

2. There are ten (oh, people) going.

3. We will leave (tomorrow, list).

4. (Today, Sleep), we will pack.

5. I make a (enough, list) of what we need.

6. I put my bag on my (today, bed).

7. I pack (enough, today) shirts.

8. I also need pants to (sleep, family) in.

9. (Oh, Enough), I have to pack socks, too!

10. If I don't remember something, I can get it
    at a (shop, tomorrow).

Name _____

Final e and Vowel Team Syllables

You can spell vowel sounds in some syllables with the vowel-consonant-*e* pattern (VC*e*), as in *placement*, or with vowel teams, as in *today*.

▶ Write each basic Spelling Word in the correct column.

Words with VCe syllables	Words with vowel team syllables
_____	_____
_____	_____
_____	_____
_____	_____
_____	_____

Spelling Words

Basic

placement
uncrate
groaning
cleanly
today
lately
unripe
decode
invite
creamy
proudly
haunting

Review

dislike
replay
unable
reread

Final e Syllables

A final *e* syllable is a syllable that has a long vowel VC*e* pattern. The word *lately* has two syllables, *late/ly*. The first syllable is a final *e* syllable, *late*. The second syllable is the suffix *–ly*.

▶ Read each word. Then write the word and draw a line to separate the syllables.

useless _____	tadpole _____
concrete _____	polite _____
wasteful _____	rotate _____

▶ Choose and write a word from above to complete each sentence. You will not use all the words.

1. It is _____ to leave water running.

2. Is it true that a _____ will grow into a frog?

3. A bucket with a hole in it is _____ .

4. Say "please" and "thank you" to be _____ .

5. The sidewalk is made of _____ .

Final e and Vowel Team Syllables

You can spell vowel sounds in some syllables with the vowel-consonant-*e* pattern (VC*e*), as in *invite*, or with vowel teams, as in *creamy*.

▶ Read each sentence. Cross out the Spelling Word that is spelled incorrectly. Write it correctly on the line.

1. The peach is unrip. _____

2. My birthday is todai. _____

3. Liz wore her ribbon prowdly. _____

4. The soup is creemy. _____

5. It has been hot laitly. _____

6. Help me uncrat the fruit. _____

7. He was growning in pain. _____

8. The story was hawnting. _____

9. I will invight you to the party. _____

▶ Write three sentences with the basic Spelling Words you did not use. Then trade with a partner. Check each other's spelling.

Spelling Words
Basic
placement
uncrate
groaning
cleanly
today
lately
unripe
decode
invite
creamy
proudly
haunting
Review
dislike
replay
unable
reread

Name _____

Phonics Review

- Look for vowel patterns when you divide longer words into syllables. The word *hopefully* has three syllables: *hope/ful/ly*. It has a final *e* syllable and two suffix syllables.

- When you add a suffix or ending to a final *e* syllable or word, you may have to make a spelling change. Drop the final *e* before adding a suffix or ending that begins with a vowel: *joke, joking, joked, joker.*

▶ Read each sentence. Write the words that have more than one syllable. Draw lines (/) to separate the syllables.

1. Dan decided to reshape his clay pot.

_____   _____

2. Carl unwisely left his coat at home on an icy day.

_____   _____

3. The broken bike lay uselessly on the ground.

_____   _____

4. John did not make a mistake when he recited the verse.

_____   _____

5. "This pie is extremely tasty!" said Lee.

_____   _____

Name _____

Words to Know

Knowing how to read and write these words can make you a better reader and writer.

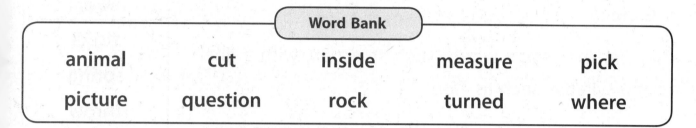

Word Bank

| animal | cut | inside | measure | pick |
| picture | question | rock | turned | where |

▶ Write a word from the box to complete each sentence. Remember to begin sentences with capital letters.

1. I will use these pens to draw a _____ .

2. Here's a _____ : What should I draw?

3. I would like to draw an _____ .

4. I will draw it next to a big _____ .

5. I will _____ out the picture.

6. I'll _____ it to see how big it is.

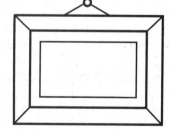

7. Then I'll put it _____ a frame.

8. _____ should I hang it?

Grade 2

309

Module 12 • Week 1

Name _____

Triple Blends; Final Stable Syllables

You can spell a word with a blend, such as *string*, by listening for the sounds of the three letters in the blend.

You can spell some words, such as *action*, with a final useful syllable, such as *–ion*.

▶ Write each basic Spelling Word in the correct box.

Basic

street

spring

throw

throat

string

spray

strong

tackle

scramble

struggle

action

picture

Review

placement

decode

proudly

haunting

Words with *str*

_____

_____

_____

_____

Words with *spr*

_____

_____

_____

_____

Words with *thr*

_____

_____

_____

Words with final useful syllables

_____

_____

_____

Name _____

Final Stable Syllables

Some syllables are useful to know. The suffixes –tion and –ture are noun-forming suffixes. Divide longer words before the suffix: action = ac/tion; creature = crea/ture.

Another useful syllable pattern is consonant + le. Divide longer words before the consonant + le: bugle = bu/gle, giggle = gig/gle.

▶ Read each word. Then write the word and draw a line to separate the syllables.

motion _____	future _____
caution _____	cuddles _____
cable _____	mixture _____

▶ Choose and write a word from above to complete each sentence. You will not use all the words.

1. The weather was a _____ of sun and clouds.

2. Grandma rocks and _____ the baby.

3. I don't know what will happen in the _____ .

4. A flashing light tells us to drive with _____ .

5. The boat floats with the _____ of the waves.

Triple Blends; Final Stable Syllables

You can spell a word with a blend, such as *throat*, by listening for the sounds of the three letters in the blend.

You can spell some words, such as *scramble*, with a final useful syllable, such as *–ble*.

▶ Read each clue. Unscramble the word. Write the Spelling Word correctly on the line.

1. Part of your body   **trahot**   _____

2. Season after winter   **rsngip**   _____

3. Not weak   **ntrsog**   _____

4. Used to tie things   **gsrnit**   _____

5. Cars drive on this   **estert**   _____

6. Draw this   **rpcitue**   _____

7. Mist   **ysrpa**   _____

8. Do this to a ball   **whrto**   _____

9. Mix up   **crsmaelb**   _____

▶ Choose other Spelling Words. Make up a clue for each one. Scramble the letters. Ask a partner to write the words correctly.

Spelling Words

Basic

street
spring
throw
throat
string
spray
strong
tackle
scramble
struggle
action
picture

Review

placement
decode
proudly
haunting

Name _____

Phonics Review

Look for final syllable patterns to help you divide longer words into syllables.

- consonant + *le* syllables: *bubble* = bub/ble; *staple* = sta/ple
- suffix *–tion*: *motion* = mo/tion; *solution* = so/lu/tion
- suffix *–ture*: *capture* = cap/ture; *adventure* = ad/ven/ture

▶ Read each sentence. Write the words with two or more syllables on the lines. Then draw a line (/) between the syllables.

1. The goat nibbles on the carnations.

_____   _____

2. The new construction is taking a long time.

_____   _____

3. Draw a picture to show the addition fact.

_____   _____

4. Max played the bugle to get our attention.

_____   _____

5. Mom bought a table and six chairs at the furniture store.

_____   _____

Name _____

Words to Know

Word Bank

America	can't	complete	easy	eyes
love	reached	sentence	state	watch

▶ Write the word from the box that best answers each clue below.

1. We use these to see. _____

2. The country where we live _____

3. I _____ my family. _____

4. Cannot _____

5. Use this to tell time. _____

6. Not hard _____

▶ Write a sentence for a word from the box you did not write yet.

_____

_____

Final Digraph/Trigraph -ch, -tch

You can spell the /ch/ sound with *ch*, as in *beach*, or with *tch*, as in *patch*.

▶ Write each basic Spelling Word in the correct column.

Words with –*ch*	Words with –*tch*
_____	_____
_____	_____
_____	_____
_____	_____
_____	_____
_____	_____

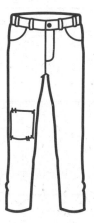

Spelling Words

Basic

itch

patch

pitch

sketch

match

ditch

catch

beach

reach

speech

coach

teacher

Review

spring

scramble

struggle

picture

Name _____

Review of Syllable Types

Divide a longer word into syllables to read it:

- V/CV pattern: Divide after the long vowel, *bonus = bo/nus*.

- VC/CV pattern: Divide between consonants, *mitten = mit/ten*.

- VCCCV pattern: Divide before consonant + *le*, *nimble = nim/ble*.

- Rule breaker: If a V/CV word does not sound right with a long vowel, divide after the consonant and try again, *seven = sev/en*.

▶ Read each sentence. Write each word with two syllables. Then draw a line (/) between the two syllables.

1. I packed the food for the picnic in a big basket.

_____   _____

2. Jan and I will work on the puzzle with the tiger.

_____   _____

3. I saw the chipmunk scramble up the tree.

_____   _____

4. I like muffins, but Dad likes donuts.

_____   _____

5. The handle on the wagon is loose.

_____   _____

Name _____

Final Digraph/Trigraph -ch, -tch

You can spell the /ch/ sound with *ch*, as in *reach*, or with *tch*, as in *patch*.

▶ Fill in the missing letters to write a Spelling Word. Then write the Spelling Word on the line.

1. bea_____   _____

2. i_____   _____

3. ske_____   _____

4. di_____   _____

5. spee_____   _____

6. tea_____er   _____

7. pi_____   _____

8. coa_____   _____

9. pa_____   _____

10. ca_____   _____

▶ Write two sentences with the basic Spelling Words you did not use. Then trade with a partner. Check each other's spelling.

Spelling Words
Basic
itch
patch
pitch
sketch
match
ditch
catch
beach
reach
speech
coach
teacher
Review
spring
scramble
struggle
picture

Phonics Review

Look for syllable types to help you divide longer words into syllables. Blend each syllable. Then connect the syllables to read the word.

- closed: *picnic = pic/nic; magnetic = mag/net/ic*
- open: *baby = ba/by; location = lo/ca/tion*
- final *e*: *excite = ex/cite; excitement = ex/cite/ment; excited = ex/cit/ed*
- *r*-controlled: *partner = part/ner; tornado = tor/na/do*
- consonant + *le*: *bubble = bub/ble; multiple = mul/ti/ple*

▶ Read each sentence. Write the words with two or more syllables on the lines. Then draw a line (/) between the syllables.

1. Mom made peanut brittle for the bake sale.

   _____   _____

2. My cellphone has a jingle for a ring tone.

   _____   _____

3. Madge likes pickles on her hamburger.

   _____   _____

4. Sam orders the homemade soup for lunch.

   _____   _____

5. Kids who misbehave at the museum must sit down.

   _____   _____

Name _____

Words to Know

Word Bank

busy	different	doing	idea	I'm
important	mind	next	plan	tried

▶ Circle the word that best completes each sentence.

1. My friend Jack has an (idea, mind).

2. He has a (busy, plan) to fix a bike.

3. He has (mind, tried) once.

4. This time, (I'm, next) going to help.

5. We will try something (plan, different).

6. We will be very (doing, busy)!

7. It is (different, important) to use good tools.

8. What will we fix (next, idea)?

Name _____

Open and Closed Syllables

You can spell a word that begins with an open syllable, such as *staple*, with a long vowel sound.

You can spell a word that begins with a closed syllable, such as *buckle*, with a short vowel sound.

▶ Write each basic Spelling Word in the correct column.

Words with open syllables	Words with closed syllables
_____	_____
_____	_____
_____	_____
_____	_____
_____	_____
_____	_____

Spelling Words

Basic

scribble

stranded

table

staple

taping

obey

playful

swimming

shady

buckle

thunder

mumble

Review

pitch

speech

reach

sketch

Name _____

Review Affixes

A *prefix* is a word part added to the beginning of a word to change its meaning. Some prefixes include *un–* (not, opposite), *re–* (again), *pre–* (before), *dis–* (not), and *mis–* (wrong, badly).

A *suffix* is a word part added to the end of a word to change its meaning. Suffixes include *–less* (without), *–ful* (full of), *–y* (like), *–ly* (in that way), *–er* (compares two), and *–est* (compares more than two).

The endings *–s* and *–es* mean "more than one" at the end of a noun. The endings *–s*, *–ed*, and *–ing* help tell when an action happens.

▶ Choose and write the word that best completes each sentence.

> **Word Bank**
>
> baking   preheated   spicy   flavorless   skillfully   misread

1. Maria wanted to make _____ meatballs.

2. She found a recipe and _____ the oven.

3. Then she _____ mixed the meat and spices.

4. Maria tasted a meatball when they finished _____ .

5. She was upset to find that they were _____ .

6. "I must have _____ the recipe," sighed Maria.

Name _____

Open and Closed Syllables

You can spell a word that begins with an open syllable, such as *table*, with a long vowel sound.

You can spell a word that begins with a closed syllable, such as *scribble*, with a short vowel sound.

▶ Write the Spelling Word that best completes each sentence.

1. The food is on the _____ .

2. You can _____ with a pen.

3. Let's sit in a _____ spot.

4. We are _____ in the pool.

5. The belt has a big _____ .

6. There was rain and _____ .

7. The kitten is _____ .

8. Please _____ the teacher.

9. You can _____ the papers together.

10. I am _____ the ripped paper.

▶ Write two more sentences like these. Then trade with a partner. Complete each other's sentences.

Spelling Words
Basic
scribble
stranded
table
staple
taping
obey
playful
swimming
shady
buckle
thunder
mumble
Review
pitch
speech
reach
sketch

Phonics Review

A *prefix* is added to the beginning of a word to change its meaning. Examples: *un*do, *re*do, **pre***heat*, **dis***like*, **mis***place*.
A *suffix* is added to the end of a word to change its meaning. Examples: *hope**less**, hope**ful**, salt**y**, quick**ly**, fast**er**, fast**est**.*

Watch for a spelling change before a suffix or ending:

- Drop final *e* before *–ed, –ing: hike, hiked, hiking.*
- Double final consonant in CVC words: *big, bigger, biggest.*
- Change *y* to *i* before *–es, –ed: hurry, hurries, hurried.*

▶ Choose and write two words to complete each sentence.

1. A smart _____ looks for _____ .

     shopping   **shopper**   **counted**   **discounts**

2. Ann _____ two words on the _____ .

     pretest   **preteen**   **misspelled**   **misstep**

3. We drove _____ on the _____ roads.

     slowly   **snowing**   **snowy**   **spoonful**

4. The _____ climbs the _____ hill.

     highest   **happier**   **hatches**   **hiker**

5. It is _____ to drink _____ water.

     unstick   **unsafe**   **salty**   **sadly**